NATURAL DEATH WITH DIGNITY:

PROTECTING YOUR RIGHT TO REFUSE MEDICAL TREATMENT
BY:
LEE R. KERR, B.S., J.D.
DELNETTA J. KERR, L.P.N.

KERR PUBLICATIONS, INC.
P.O. BOX 352
HYSHAM MT 59038

First Printing 1991
Second Printing 1991
Published in the United States by
Kerr Publications, Inc.
P.O. Box 352
Hysham, MT 59038-0352

Publisher's Cataloging in Publication
(Prepared by Quality Books Inc.)

Kerr, Lee R., 1954-
   Natural death with dignity : protecting your right to refuse
medical treatment / by Lee R. Kerr, Delnetta J. Kerr. --
   p. cm.
   Includes the full text of the U.S. Supreme Court decision in the
case of Cruzan v. Missouri.
   Includes bibliographical references and index.
   ISBN 0-9628237-0-8
   ISBN 0-962837-1-6 Hard Cover
   1. Right to die--Law and legislation--United States. 2. Informed
consent (Medical law)--United States. 3. Holland, Phyllis. 4.
Cruzan, Nancy Beth--Trials, litigation, etc. I. Kerr, Delnetta J.
II. Title.

KF3827.E87   334.73'0419
                                     QBI90-187

DEDICATION

This book is dedicated to the loving memory of Phyllis and Eugene Holland, whose quiet pain and suffering was the inspiration for this book. Phyllis, a WWII veteran, was a loving, devoted wife and mother, who was taken from her family by a degenerative neurological disease. As Phyllis' condition deteriorated, she had to leave her husband and two small children, committing herself to a veterans hospital in anticipation of her own death.

Unfortunately, the wait was torturous in length, and Phyllis deteriorated slowly over the course of thirty years (yes, 30 years!). Phyllis' last seventeen years of physical existence was spent in a progressively comatose state while being provided extensive acute medical care, including surgically implanted tube feedings and hydration. Phyllis never would have wanted this, but neither she nor her family knew anything else was possible. After thirty tortured years, with the insistence of the family, legal counsel, and cooperation of sympathetic medical professionals, Phyllis was finally allowed to die.

Through all these years, her devoted husband, Eugene, remained faithful to her, raised their two small children and maintained his own quiet tortured vigil; waiting, waiting, for his wife's passing. Eugene, or "Red" as his friends and family called him, near the end of Phyllis' life, learned about a new kind of legal document called a "living will", which he had prepared for himself and executed.

Shortly after Phyllis passed away, "Red", who had suffered several "small" strokes over the years during his vigil, suffered a massive stroke, with a resultant extreme high fever, and lapsed into a deep coma. "Red's" attending physician was made aware of what "Red" would want under these circumstances, and was given a copy of "Red's" "living will". As a result, no heroic or unwanted medical care was provided, and "Red" passed away quietly in a few days. This loving husband, father, and decorated veteran from World War II had, "done his duty". The vigil was over. "Red" was finally at peace.

IMPORTANT NOTICE

While every possible effort has been made to ensure the accuracy of the information in this book, the Editors of this book, the publisher, and the authors, reviewers, and consultants do not accept responsibility for any misinterpretation or misapplication by the reader of the information contained in this book. This book is designed to provide information in regard to the subject matter covered. The forms contained in this book will be subject to applicable laws, which could vary significantly from state to state or change over time. The publishing of this book does not constitute the practice of law, nor does it attempt to provide legal advice concerning any specific factual situation. This book is not a substitute for any attorney, nor does it attempt to answer all questions about all situations you may encounter. The Editors of this book advise the reader to consult an attorney for appropriate advice on specific legal problems as circumstances dictate.

NATURAL DEATH WITH DIGNITY:

PROTECTING YOUR RIGHT TO REFUSE MEDICAL TREATMENT

CONTENTS:

NATURAL DEATH WITH DIGNITY:

PROTECTING YOUR RIGHT TO REFUSE MEDICAL TREATMENT

CHAPTER 1 —

INTRODUCTION

There is an evil specter hanging over America. The evil specter is the potential stripping away and violation of your most basic privacy and liberty interests in controlling your own body. It is perpetrated by the medical profession by the providing of unwanted or unneeded medical care to many who have lost the capacity to refuse what may be well intended, but misguided, care.

Ideally, you would probably choose to live out your days in peace, hoping to live a full and active life, and to quietly pass away in your sleep at the end of a full and productive life. Unfortunately, this is not the case for many Americans. Thousands upon thousands die each year only after long and protracted illnesses, with slow and agonizing deaths. This book may very well be the most important book you will ever read in your life, if it successfully helps you to adequately prepare for the eventuality of your own incapacity and death. This book will provide you with the information and tools you need to make adequate advanced preparation, so you might retain your individual dignity, and be allowed to finish your life without unreasonable or intrusive interference by the medical profession.

The medical profession is normally not perceived as your enemy. Yet, if you are unfortunate enough to reach the point in your existence where you are incompetent and incapable of making your own decisions, then the medical profession may well become your worst nightmare. The medical profession in recent years has made great strides in advancements in medical technology, giving them a vast array of tools, including medications, devices and techniques to prolong your physical existence far longer than was ever previously possible. This vast array of resources the medical profession can now draw upon to extend your life far beyond what you may reasonably wish it to be extended is brought upon by many factors. First, american society has become very litigious, and medical providers often have the reaction that if they have the technical capacity to maintain a human existence, they need to reduce their exposure from liability by providing all care they are technically capable of providing. In some cases, physicians also fear criminal prosecution, believing withdrawal or refusal to provide care to be equivalent to euthanasia. Ironically, the vast majority of litigation pertains to loved ones and relatives attempting to obtain a legal order to have care withheld, rather than any suit or prosecution for damages because care was not provided. An excruciatingly painful case history is documented well in the recent Supreme Court <u>Cruzan</u> Decision, which is set out in its entirety in Chapter 3 of this book.

The second most significant factor that drives the desire and objective to provide undesired, unneeded, health care, which is far more sinister and seldom talked about, is the mega dollar economic factor in providing hi-tech care. In the same way some physicians and health care providers order unnecessary or unneeded diagnostic tests to protect themselves from liability, others will order unnecessary tests simply to increase their profits. This same problem exists in the care of incompetent patients. Massive profits are derived from maintaining patients on expensive hi-tech equipment. It is an extremely difficult and sensitive subject matter, and often impossible to prove. You do not want to believe that care is provided for the sake of money and greed. Yet, it would be extremely naive to believe it does not occur, and occur frequently.

The bottom line: If there is ever any doubt an available medical procedure or technique should be utilized to maintain your physical existence, be assured it will be utilized and applied, unless your desires and intentions to not receive this care are expressly and clearly made available and known to your health care providers. If you should become incompetent, either suddenly or otherwise, you must make advanced preparations so your intent and instructions are followed regarding your desires for medical care.

The purpose of this book is quite simply to provide you the information and skills you need to avoid a potential living hell for you and your family. This book addresses the subject matter of living wills and related topics. If you have already prepared a living will or have already heard about living wills, please read on. The recent Supreme Court Cruzan case, has added additional dimensions to living wills, and increased their importance. More importantly, the Cruzan case has recognized a constitutional right to refuse medical treatment. This has previously always been thought to exist by most legal commentators. However, this right has only now been first expressly recognized by the United States Supreme Court in Cruzan. Further, since the Supreme Court has recognized a state's right to require medical treatment, unless there is clear and convincing evidence of the intent of the patient to not receive certain medical care, it is all the more important living wills and related documents be drafted with a great deal of clarity and precision. These properly drafted documents will provide "clear and convincing" evidence to health care professionals and the legal system, if necessary. Although your State in the future may not mandate as high a legal standard of proof as is currently required in Missouri, but can you afford to take that chance?

The authors also recognize a growing controversy in this country surrounding basic issues dealing with the sanctity and protection of life. Moralistic and religious fervor have embroiled these issues, and the factions have generally been categorized as either pro-life or pro-choice. It is not this book's intent to support or oppose either one of these factions. Nor is there any intent to support or encourage euthanasia. This book's simple intent is to give you the knowledge and resources to protect your federal constitutional right to refuse medical treatment. Thus, as you complete the steps outlined in this book, you are then equipped to protect or enforce your own moral code or religious beliefs in a dignified manner, without unwanted intrusion by medical technology.

In furtherance of these goals, this book instructs you in a basic three step approach that should be complied with to help adequately insure your intentions will be followed regarding medical care. The next chapter explains our personal experiences and background so you might better understand the need and urgency for advanced planning. We also provide you the entire text of the Supreme Court Cruzan Decision so you may have a greater understanding and awareness of both the human tragedies that can develop, and also an appreciation for the legal complexities involved.

Then, you are instructed in our recommended three step process, which comprises of , (1) complying with your own state's statutory living will laws, (2) drafting your own detailed personal declaration of intent regarding limiting medical consent, and (3) preparing a durable power of attorney for limiting or refusing medical consent.

Many readers may not have heard of living wills before, or have only had some perception because of the recent publicity of the Cruzan Case. It is to those people this book attempts to principally speak. Further, there are many of you who have had some exposure to living wills, and perhaps may have prepared some simple form provided to you by some organization or group. If you have been provided a simple form and simply filled it out and had it signed and witnessed, we encourage you to think again and follow through the process provided for in this book. In light of Cruzan, this is not a simple issue and you must guard against an overly simplistic solution. The issues are complex and require some effort in understanding and familiarizing yourself with them. You need to be adequately informed so that you can prepare an issue directives that will address the necessary issues, and be sufficiently clear and complete to provide the level of evidence necessary to ultimately enforce your directives.

Having said that, do not be discouraged or put off. The few hours you are going to spend going through the materials in this book and preparing the necessary documents may be the most important hours you ever spend in your life.

NATURAL DEATH WITH DIGNITY:

PROTECTING YOUR RIGHT TO REFUSE MEDICAL TREATMENT

CHAPTER 2 —

OUR STORY

Undoubtedly one of the first questions to cross your mind is, what motivated us to write this book? As it may have become obvious to you from the dedication to this book and the comment about the authors, we have been inspired by a personal tragedy in our own family, not unlike that experienced by the Cruzans or the Karen Ann Quinlan family, or thousands of others occuring each year in this country. Perhaps our family tragedy was worse in some ways than the numerous cases appearing across the country in the legal digests and reporters. In most of these reported cases there usually is an effort to stop or terminate medical care so a loved one may be permitted to die with some semblance of dignity.   In the Quinlan and Cruzan cases, the tragedy the legal action was attempting to prevent, was potential years of maintenance of a comatose patient, often on tube feedings and hydration, when that patient, if able to say no more, would say no more.   In our family's case, the tragedy began over thirty years ago before the emergence of any of this new case law development, or concepts of living wills, or powers of attorneys for medical consent.   Although these concepts undoubtedly existed, there certainly was not a body of case law to support them, nor was the availability of such options commonly distributed or made available to our family.

Thus, our family has lived out the tragedy the Quinlan and Cruzan court actions sought to prevent. Phyllis Holland, Delnetta Kerr's mother, spent thirty years institutionalized, in the process of dying, from the degenerative neurological disease "Huntington's Chorea". The last seventeen years of which were spent in a semi-comatose to comatose state, on tube feedings and hydration. Neither Phyllis nor the family knew anything about living wills or powers of attorney for medical consent. Phyllis' two brothers were afflicted with the same disease and had died after contracting the disease. Phyllis anticipated dying within a relatively short period of time and had committed herself to the Veteran's Hospital on the anticipation of death. However, Phyllis had the tragic distinction of physically existing longer than other previously diagnosed Huntington's Chorea patients. After thirty years of institutional care, that no one could have anticipated or predicted, Phyllis was quietly allowed to die. This was made possible only by very recent case law developments in the state in which Phyllis was institutionalized, which allowed for the termination of tube feedings, if numerous criteria and procedures were followed. The procedures were followed and the tube feeding was discontinued, allowing Phyllis to finally rest, and the nightmare to end for our family. You can avoid this type of tragedy for yourself and your family if you follow the information and instructions provided for in this book.

What follows is co-author Delnetta Kerr's own personal statement and appeal to you directly to give you a greater understanding of the tragedy you and your family might experience if you do not take the appropriate advanced planning steps now to prevent such a tragedy:

"I remember very little of my very young childhood and very little of my grade school years, one to six. When I was approximately five years old, thirty years ago, mother was forced to leave her beloved family and home, due to an illness called Huntington's Chorea. First she committed herself to the State Mental Hospital while waiting to be accepted at a Veteran's Administration Hospital, since she had been a Wave in the Navy during World War II. Mother committed herself to protect her family because her mental and physical condition was declining, from the progressive nature of the disease. In the beginning, every chance we got we took the train to see mother, it was a one and one-half day trip by train. Mother's instructions were very clear. Once she no longer knew us, we were to no longer come to visit her, as it would be of no benefit to her, and it would be very devastating to all of us. Father was a very loving and caring man who only wanted to care for his family, and took mother's illness very hard.

As time went on mother did not know who any of us were, my brother five years elder, my father, or myself. I can't remember exactly when we stopped going, but we did as it was destroying the rest of us, and mother had left her instructions. The woman in the Veteran's Hospital was no longer mother, she had become some strange woman who looked similar to mother.

As the years went by we talked very little about mother. Father was willing to talk, but I could see the pain in his eyes when we spoke of her, so I never asked. Father was a very special person loved by most everyone who knew him. He was a better parent than most two parents together. He was always there when I needed him, and I could talk to him about anything, there was no generation gap between us. As the years passed, mother became less and less responsive, and finally after twelve years, she was in a coma like state unable to feed, cloth, or even turn herself in bed. She had become completely unresponsive.

At that time, the Veteran's Administration Hospital began tube feedings and hydration. Father had no choice in the matter, no one had ever heard of anything like a "living will" or knew it was possible to refuse to receive this kind of medical treatment. Approximately three years after they began the tube feedings, father began having strokes affecting his right side. He was also a veteran and entered a Veteran's Hospital. After four months of treatment, he was released to come home. His speech was badly affected as was his right arm. Just prior to father's illness, my uncle passed away of Huntington's Chorea. He was mother's younger brother. Father was the guardian of mother and my uncle. As he became unable to perform his duties due to his own illness, he asked me to become mother's guardian and personal representative of my uncle's estate. I was twenty-one years old at the time. I, of course, did as my father asked and became mother's guardian and personal representative of my Uncle's estate. My Uncle's closest living relative was mother, as their older brother had passed away of Huntington's Chorea earlier. My uncle had no heirs, and both grandparents were gone also. I believe grandmother passed away in a mental institution of dancer's disease, (another name for Huntington's

Chorea, an old layman's term).

While institutionalized, mother was in many medical studies, and was even filmed in a medical documentary, which was never used, in Huntington's Chorea research. I had always been opposed to her being kept alive by artificial means, but was unable to discontinue it. Why it was ever begun I will never understand.

Two years ago I received a call from the Veterans Administration asking if I would be opposed to mother being moved out of the Veteran's Hospital to a nursing home. I asked why after twenty-eight years would there be a reason to move her. I was told the room she was in could be used for two men instead of one woman and some drug manufacturer was going to fund a study on alzheimer's disease so they wanted the room for that. I refused permission to move her. Soon after, the V. A. started full scale to arrange to get mother out of the Veteran's Hospital. Their reasoning then was she was stable and did not need hospital care but needed convalescent care. Her condition had been basically the same for the past ten years. She now had been on tube feedings for sixteen years. I had to hire an attorney to help. As previously indicated, I was opposed to tube feedings and had wanted to let mother pass away, as she had intended when she was unable to feed herself or even eat food someone else fed her. Since I live in one state and my mother was hospitalized in another, I soon had to employ a second attorney in the other state. The attorney, while researching the law, discovered new legal decisions which would allow for the removal of tube feedings in the terminally ill if certain conditions were met. I was also told if "living wills" were known about when mother fell ill and had executed one, years of tube feedings in a coma like state could of been avoided.

The Veteran's Administration refused to follow the family's written instructions to discontinue the tube feedings and continued to attempt to find a nursing home that would accept mother. Finally, they found one that would take her. They did not notify me of her transfer until after she had been transferred. Mother was considered a very difficult patient as she had to be turned every two hours. Her skin had to be taken very good care of, and many precautions had to be taken to prevent skin break down and infection. The expense for this kind of nursing care is expensive and I was worried how my 74 year old father would be able to care for mother once guardianship money was exhausted.

After one and one-half years of legal fighting, seventeen years of tube feedings, multiple exams from other Doctors evaluating her condition, an evaluation by the church, a total of almost 30 years in the V. A. Hospital and other hospitals elsewhere, mother's tube feedings were discontinued and she was finally allowed to die with some dignity. She was finally allowed to have her final rest and peace. Finally, seventeen years after the tube feedings began the family was able to have them removed to allow mother to pass away as I believe God had intended seventeen years before. Mother had no will or written instructions. We only knew her wishes, which were not to be kept alive artificially. Nearly thirty years of heartache, seventeen of which should never have occurred. If only she could have signed a "living will" or even a durable power of attorney for medical consent, so much pain, heartache, and frustration could have been avoided.

Soon after mother passed away, father became critically ill from a massive stroke. Fourteen years earlier he had suffered right sided strokes and had difficulty using his right arm and had impaired speech. He also over the years after his strokes had three heart attacks. Yet, he was still mentally sharp as a tack, and when he learned about "living wills", he had one prepared which he signed. During his final hospitalization, he slipped into a coma. The Doctors told us father had no reasonable chance of recovery from the coma but could be maintained artificially on a ventilator. We gave his doctor his signed "living will" which stated his wishes as to not being kept alive by artificial means if he had a terminal condition. After medical testing, it was found he had experienced another stroke, only on the left side this time. As his "living will" dictated, no artificial means of life support was used. He passed quietly away in less than one week, never awakening from the coma.

I truly hope the following pages and instructions will prevent you from having the nightmare my family and I have had to go through. I believe that had mother had available and had signed a "living will" prior to her onset of illness, father would be here today. He would not have had seventeen years of heartache, pain, and regret. He would have been free to begin a new life. You see, father remained true over all the years to mother and his beloved wife.

Please protect your rights, the rights of your family, and possibly the financial security of your family. Prevent the long term heartache and pain. This has all been done in the memory of my beloved parents and in the hope none of you will be forced to endure the pain they had endured, or the pain endured by my entire family. Please make your intentions clear, to your loved ones and your health care professionals. Make the decisions for yourself, don't force your loved ones to make the decision for you. The law may not even allow them to. After long talks with my father and brother, and knowing this was what mother wanted, signing the papers to have the tube feedings discontinued was still one of the hardest things I have ever done. The only thing father wanted was for mother to finally be at rest. We finally completed the task. I hope our story and the following information will help you complete your task, so a loved one won't have to.

To help guide you, we are providing you with the following information. Please review this information carefully and act now to protect yourself and your family."

15

NATURAL DEATH WITH DIGNITY:

PROTECTING YOUR RIGHT TO REFUSE MEDICAL TREATMENT

CHAPTER 3 —

THE CRUZAN CASE

We have decided to provide you the entire U.S. Supreme Court Decision, Cruzan v. Missouri, for two basic reasons. First, it provides an excellent additional case history of what can go wrong if adequate preparation is not made. It is a legal "Horror" story in the truest sense of the word. The second reason is the legal discussion familiarizes the reader with the complex issues involved, and clarifies the critical need for every American competent to understand the issues to draft a statutory living will, a personal statement of intent regarding refusing or limiting medical consent, and a durable power of attorney for medical care.

For those readers not familiar with reading legal opinions, the majority opinion, located at the beginning of the opinion by Chief Justice Rehnquist, and signed by Justices White, O'Connor, Scalia, and Kennedy, is the "Law of the Land". It is controlling legal authority for lower courts and the Supreme Court, unless overruled by the Supreme Court at a later date. The concurring opinions of Justices O'Connor and Scalia, indicate they agree in the result, but for either different or additional reasons, which they express in their separate written opinions.

A dissenting opinion follows the majority and concurring opinions, which was written by Justice Brennan, and which Justices Marshall and Blackmun agreed with. A dissenting opinion is not "Law", but a written opinion by the Justices who did not vote for the majority opinion as to why they disagreed with the majority opinion. Justice Stevens also filed a separate dissenting opinion. Four Justices strongly believed there had been sufficient proof Nancy Cruzan would not want to be kept alive by tube feedings in her present condition and should be allowed to die.

However, this was not enough, and the other five Justices majority decision held that Nancy Cruzan's family had not met their burden of proof of "clear and convincing" evidence. Nancy Cruzan had no living will. So long as Nancy Cruzan continued to remain in Missouri and the Missouri legislature did not change Missouri law, Nancy Cruzan's family would have to meet this very high burden of proof or Nancy would continue to be "tube fed" in a persistent vegetative state for the remainder of her physical existence, even if she continued for the next thirty years.

After the Supreme Court issued its decision, attorneys for the Cruzans went back to court in Missouri to present additional evidence from friends and co-workers about Nancy's intentions regarding health care, to meet this high burden of proof imposed by Missouri, and upheld by the Supreme Court. A Missouri Court finally decided the burden had been met and ordered the tube feedings stopped. Shortly thereafter, the tube feedings were stopped and Nancy Cruzan was allowed to quietly pass away, Wednesday, December 26th, 1990, 12 days after the feeding tube that had kept her in a vegetative state for eight years was removed.

No. 88-1503

NANCY BETH CRUZAN, By her Parents and Co-Guardians, LESTER L. CRUZAN, ET UX., PETITIONERS v. DIRECTOR, MISSOURI DEPARTMENT OF HEALTH, ET AL.

ON WRIT OF CERTIORARI TO THE SUPREME COURT OF MISSOURI

DECIDED: JUNE 25, 1990

REHNQUIST, C.J., delivered the opinion of the Court, in which WHITE, O'CONNOR, SCALIA, and KENNEDY, JJ., joined. O'CONNOR, J., and SCALIA, L., filed concurring opinions. BRENNAN, J., filed a dissenting opinion, in which MARSHALL and BLACKMUN, JJ., joined. STEVENS, J., filed a dissenting opinion.

CHIEF JUSTICE REHNQUIST delivered the opinion of the Court.

(Editor's Note-This is the majority opinion-the "LAW OF THE LAND")

Petitioner Nancy Beth Cruzan was rendered incompetent as a result of severe injuries sustained during an automobile accident. Co-petitioners Lester and Joyce Cruzan, Nancy's parents and co-guardians, sought a court order directing the withdrawal of their daughter's artificial feeding and hydration equipment after it became apparent that she had virtually no chance of recovering her cognitive faculties. The Supreme Court of Missouri held that because there was no clear and convincing evidence of Nancy's desire to have life-sustaining treatment withdrawn under such circumstances, her parents lacked authority to effectuate such a request. We granted certiorari, 492 U.S. _____ (1989), and now affirm.

On the night of January 11, 1983, Nancy Cruzan lost control of her car as she traveled down Elm Road in Jasper County, Missouri, The vehicle overturned, and Cruzan was discovered lying down in a ditch without detectable respiratory or cardiac function. Paramedics were able to restore her breathing and heartbeat at the accident site, and she was transported to a hospital in an unconscious state. An attending neurosurgeon diagnosed her as having sustained probable cerebral contusions compounded by significant anoxia (lack of oxygen). The Missouri trial court in this case found that permanent brain damage generally results after 6 minutes in an anoxic state; it was estimated that Cruzan was deprived of oxygen from 12 to 14 minutes. She remained in a coma for approximately three weeks and then progressed to an unconscious state in which she was able to orally ingest some nutrition. In order to ease feeding and further the recovery, surgeons implanted a gastrostomy feeding and hydration tube in Cruzan with the consent of her then husband. Subsequent rehabilitative efforts proved unavailing. She now lies in a Missouri state hospital in what is commonly referred to as a persistent vegetative state: generally, a condition in which a person exhibits motor reflexes but evinces no indications of significant cognitive function.[1] The State of Missouri is bearing the cost of her care.

After it had become apparent that Nancy Cruzan had virtually no chance of regaining her mental faculties her parents asked hospital employees to terminate the artificial nutrition and hydration procedures. All agree that such a removal would cause her death. The employees refused to honor the request without court approval. The parents then sought and received authorization from the state trial court for termination. The court found that a person in Nancy's condition had a fundamental right under the State and Federal Constitutions to refuse or direct the withdrawal of "death prolonging procedures." App. to Pet. for Cert. A99. The court also found that Nancy's "expressed thoughts at age twenty-five in somewhat serious conversation with a housemate friend that if sick or injured she would not wish to continue her life unless she could live at least halfway normally suggests that given her present condition she would not wish to continue on with her nutrition and hydration. Id., at A97-A98.

The Supreme Court of Missouri reversed by a divided vote. The court recognized a right to refuse treatment embodied in the common-law doctrine of informed consent, but expressed skepticism about the application of that doctrine in the circumstances of this case. Cruzan v. Harmon, 760 S.W. 2d 408, 416-417 (Mo. 1988) (enbanc). The court also declined to read a broad right of privacy into the State Constitution which should "support the right of a person to refuse medical treatment in every circumstance," and expressed doubt as to whether such a right existed under the United States Constitution. Id., at 417-418. It then decided that the Missouri Living Will statute, Mo. Rev. Stat. Section 459.010 et seq. (1986), embodied a state policy strongly favoring the preservation of life. 760 S.W. 2d, at 419-420. The court found that Cruzan's statements to her roommate regarding her desire to live or die under certain conditions were "unreliable for the purpose of determining her intent," id., at 424, "and thus insufficient to support the co-guardians claim to exercise substituted judgment on Nancy's behalf." Id., at 426. It rejected the argument that Cruzan's parents were entitled to order the termination of her medical treatment, concluding that "no person can assume that choice for an incompetent in the absence of the formalities required under Missouri's Living Will statutes or the clear and convincing, inherently reliable evidence absent here." Id., at 425. The court also expressed its view that "[b]road policy questions bearing on life and death are more properly addressed by representative assemblies" than judicial bodies. Id., at 426.

We granted certiorari to consider the question of whether Cruzan has a right under the United States Constitution which would require the hospital to withdraw life-sustaining treatment from her under these circumstances.

At common law, even the touching of one person by another without consent and without legal justification was a battery. See W. Keeton, D. Dobbs, R. Keeton, & D. Owen, Prosser and Keeton on Law of Torts Section 9, pp. 39-42 (5th ed. 1984). Before the turn of the century, this Court observed that "[n]o right is held more sacred, or is more carefully guarded, by the common law, than the right of every individual to the possession and control of his own person, free from all restraint or interference of others, unless by clear and unquestionable authority of law." Union Pacific R. Co. v. Botsford, 141 U.S. 250, 251 (1891). This notion of bodily integrity has been embodied in the requirement that informed consent is generally required for medical treatment. Justice Cardozo, while on the Court of Appeals of New York, aptly described this doctrine: "every human being of adult years and sound mind has a right to determine what shall be done with his own body; and a surgeon who performs an operation without his patient's consent commits an assault, for which he is liable in damages." Schloendorff v. Society of New York Hospital, 211 N.Y. 125, 129-30, 105 N.E. 92, 93 (1914). The informed consent doctrine has become firmly entrenched in American tort law. See Dobbs, Keeton, & Owen, supra, Section 32, pp. 189-192; F. Rozovsky, Consent to Treatment, A Practical Guide 1-998 (2d ed. 1990).

The logical corollary of the doctrine of informed consent is that the patient generally possesses the right not to consent, that is, to refuse treatment. Until about 15 years ago and the seminal decision in In re Quinlan, 70 N.J. 10, 355 A. 2d 647, cert. denied sub nom., Garger v. New Jersey, 429 U.S. 922 (1976), the number of right-to-refuse-treatment decisions were relatively few.[2] Most of the earlier cases involved patients who refused medical treatment forbidden by their religious beliefs, thus implicating First Amendment rights as well as common law rights of self-determination.[3] More recently, however, with the advance of medical technology capable of sustaining life well past the point where natural forces would have brought certain death in earlier times, cases involving the right to refuse life-sustaining treatment have burgeoned. See 760 S.W. 2d, at 412, n. 4 (collecting 54 reported decisions from 1976-1988).

In the Quinlan case, young Karen Quinlan suffered severe brain damage as the result of anoxia, and entered a persistent vegetative state. Karen's father sought judicial approval to disconnect his daughter's respirator. The New Jersey supreme Court granted the relief, holding that Karen had a right of privacy grounded in the Federal Constitution to terminate treatment. In re Quinlan, 70 N.J., at 38-42, 355 A. 2d at 662-664. Recognizing that this right was not absolute, however, the court balanced it against asserted state interests. Noting that the State's interest "weakens and the individual's right to privacy grows as the degree of bodily invasion increases and the prognosis dims," the court concluded that the state interests had to give way in that case. Id., at 41, 355 A. 2d, at 664. The court also concluded that the "only practical way" to prevent the loss of Karen's privacy right due to her incompetence was to allow her guardian and family to decide "whether she would exercise it in these circumstances." Ibid.

After Quinlan, however, most courts have based a right to refuse treatment either solely on the common law right to informed consent or on both the common law right and a constitutional privacy right. See L. Tribe, American Constitutional Law Section 15-11, p. 1365 (2d ed. 1988). In Superintendent of Belchertown State School v. Saikewicz, 373 Mass. 728, 370 N.E. 2d 417 (1977), the Supreme Judicial Court of Massachusetts relied on both the right of privacy and the right of informed consent to permit the withholding of chemotherapy from a profoundly-retarded 67-year-old man suffering from leukemia. Id., at 737-738, 370 N.E. 2d, at 424. Reasoning that an incompetent person retains the same rights as a competent individual "because the value of human dignity extends to both," the court adopted a "substituted judgment" standard whereby courts were to determine what an incompetent individual's decision would have been under the circumstances. Id., at 745, 752-753, 757-758, 370 N.E. 2d, at 427, 431, 434. Distilling certain state interests from prior case law - the preservation of life, the protection of the interests of innocent third parties, the prevention of suicide, and the maintenance of the ethical integrity of the medical profession - the court recognized the first interest as paramount and noted it was greatest when an affliction was curable, "as opposed to the State interest where, as here, the issue is not whether, but when, for how long, and at what cost to the individual [a] life may be briefly extended." Id., at 742, 370 N.E. 2d, at 426.

In In re Storar 52 N.Y. 2d 363, 420 N.E. 2d 64, cert. denied, 454 U.S. 858 (1981), the New York Court of Appeals declined to base a right to refuse treatment on a constitutional privacy right. Instead, it found such a right "adequately supported" by the informed consent doctrine. Id., at 376-377, 420 N.E. 2d, at 70. In In re Eichner (decided with In re Storar, supra) an 83-year-old man who had suffered brain damage from anoxia entered a vegetative state and was thus incompetent to consent to the removal of his respirator. The court, however, found it unnecessary to reach the question of whether his rights could be exercised by others since it found the evidence clear and convincing from statements made by the patient when competent that he "did not want to be maintained in a vegetative coma by use of a respirator." Id., at 380, 420 N.E. 2d, at 72. In the companion Storar case, a 52-year-old man suffering from bladder cancer had been profoundly retarded during most of his life. Implicitly rejecting the approach taken in Saikewicz, supra, the court reasoned that due to such life-long incompetency, "it is unrealistic to attempt to determine whether he would want to continue potentially life prolonging treatment if he were competent." 52 N.Y. 2d, at 380, 420 N.E. 2d, at 72. As the evidence showed that the patient's required blood transfusions did not involve excessive pain and without them his mental and physical abilities would deteriorate, the court concluded that it should not "allow an incompetent patient to bleed to death because someone, even someone as close as a parent or sibling, feels that this is best for one with an incurable disease." Id., at 382, 420 N.E. 2d, at 73.

Many of the later cases build on the principles established in Quinlan, Saikewicz, and Storar/Eichner. For instance, in In re Conroy, 98 N.J. 321, 486 A 2d 1209 (1985), the same court that decided Quinlan considered whether a nasogastric feeding tube could be removed from an 84-year-old incompetent nursing-home resident suffering irreversible mental and physical ailments. While recognizing that a federal right of privacy might apply in the case, the court, contrary to its approach in Quinlan, decided to base its decision on the common-law right to self-determination and informed consent. 98 N.J., at 348, 486 A 2d, at 1223. "On balance, the right to self-determination ordinarily outweighs any countervailing state interests, and competent persons generally are permitted to refuse medical treatment, even at the risk involved the interest in protecting innocent third parties, have concerned the patient's competency to make a rational and considered choice." Id., at 353-354, 486 A. 2d, at 1225.

Reasoning that the right of self-determination should not be lost merely because an individual is unable to sense a violation of it, the court held that incompetent individuals retain a right to refuse treatment. It also held that such a right could be exercised by a surrogate decisionmaker using a "subjective" standard when there was clear evidence that the incompetent person would have exercised it. Where such evidence was lacking, the court held that an individual's right could still be invoked in certain circumstances under objective "best interest" standards. Id., at 361-368, 486 A. 2d, at 1229-1233. Thus, if some trustworthy evidence existed that the individual would have wanted to terminate treatment, but not enough to clearly establish a person's wishes for purposes of the subjective standard, and the burden of a prolonged life from the experience of pain and suffering markedly outweighed its satisfactions, treatment could be terminated under a "limited-objective" standard. Where no trustworthy evidence existed, and a person's suffering would make the administration of life-sustaining treatment inhumane, a "pure-objective" standard could be used to terminate treatment. If none of these conditions obtained, the court held it was best to err in favor of preserving life. Id., at 364-368, 486 A. 2d, at 1231-1233.

The court also rejected certain categorical distinctions that had been drawn in prior refusal-of-treatment cases as lacking substance for decision purposes: the distinction between actively hastening death by terminating treatment and passively allowing a person to die of a disease; between treating individuals as an initial matter versus withdrawing treatment afterwards; between ordinary versus extraordinary treatment; and between treatment by artificial feeding versus other forms of life-sustaining medical procedures. Id., at 369-374, 486 N.E. 2d, at 1233-1237. As to the last item, the court acknowledged the "emotional significance" of food, but noted that feeding by implanted tubes is a "medical procedur[e] with inherent risks and possible side effects, instituted by skilled health-care providers to compensate for impaired physical functioning" which analytically was equivalent to artificial breathing using a respirator. Id., at 373, 486 A. 2d, at 1236.[4]

In contrast to Conroy, the Court of Appeals of New York recently refused to accept less than the clearly expressed wishes of a patient before permitting the exercise of her right to refuse treatment by a surrogate decisionmaker. In re Westchester county Medical Center on behalf of O'Connor, 531 N.E. 2d 607 (1988) (O'Connor). There, the court, over the objection of the patient's family members, granted an order to insert a feeding tube into a 77-year-old woman rendered incompetent as a result of several strokes. While continuing to recognize a common-law right to refuse treatment, the court rejected the substituted judgment approach for asserting it "because it is inconsistent with our fundamental commitment to the notion that no person or court should substitute its judgment as to what would be an acceptable quality of life for another. Consequently, we adhere to the view that, despite its pitfalls and inevitable uncertainties, the

23

inquiry must always be narrowed to the patient's expressed intent, with every effort made to minimize the opportunity for error." Id., at 530, 531 N.E. 2d, at 613 (citation omitted). The court held that the record lacked the requisite clear and convincing evidence of the patient's expressed intent to withhold life-sustaining treatment. Id., at 531-534, 531 N.E. 2d, at 613-615.

Other courts have found state statutory law relevant to the resolution of these issues. In Conservatorship of Drabick, 200 Cal. App. 3d 185, 245 Cal. Rptr. 840, cert. denied, _____ U.S. _____ (1988), the California Court of Appeal authorized the removal of a nasogastric feeding tube from a 44-year-old man who was in a persistent vegetative state as a result of an auto accident. Noting that the right to refuse treatment was grounded in both the common law and a constitutional right of privacy, the court held that a state probate statute authorized the patient's conservator to order the withdrawal of life-sustaining treatment when such a decision was made in good faith based on medical advise and the conservatee's best interests. While acknowledging that "to claim that [a patient's] 'right to choose' survives incompetence is a legal fiction at best," the court reasoned that the respect society accords to persons as individuals is not lost upon incompetence and is best preserved by allowing others "to make a decision that reflects [a patient's] interests more closely than would a purely technological decision to do whatever is possible."[5] Id., at 208, 245 Cal. Rptr., at 854-855. See also In re Conservatorship of Torres, 357 N.W. 2d 332 (Minn. 1984) (Minnesota court had constitutional and statutory authority to authorize a conservator to order the removal of an incompetent individual's respirator since in patient's best interests).

In In re Estate of Longeway, 123 Ill. 2d 33, 549 N.E. 2d 292 (1989), the Supreme Court of Illinois considered whether a 76-year-old woman rendered incompetent from a series of strokes had a right to the discontinuance of artificial nutrition and hydration. Noting that the boundaries of a federal right of privacy were uncertain, the court found a right to refuse treatment in the doctrine of informed consent. Id., 15 43-45, 549 N.E. 2d, at 296-297. The court further held that the State Probate Act impliedly authorized a guardian to exercise a ward's right to refuse artificial sustenance in the event that the ward was terminally ill and irreversibly comatose. Id., at 15-46, 549 N.E. 2d, at 298. Declining to adopt a best interests standard for deciding when it would be appropriate to exercise a ward's right because it "lets another make a determination of a patient's quality of life," the court opted instead for a substituted judgment standard. Id., at 49, 549 N.E. 2d, at 299. Finding the "expressed intent" standard utilized in O'Connor, supra, too rigid, the court noted that other clear and convincing evidence of the patient's intent could be considered. 133 Ill. 2d, at 50-51, 549 N.E. 2d, at 300. The court also adopted the "consensus opinion [that] treats artificial nutrition and hydration as medical treatment." Id., at 42, 549 N.E. 2d, at 296. Cf. McConnell v. Beverly Enterprises-Connecticut, Inc., 209 Conn. 692, 705, 553 A. 2d 596, 603 (1989) (right to withdraw artificial nutrition and hydration found in the Connecticut Removal of Life support Systems Act, which "provid[es] functional guidelines for the exercise of the common law and constitutional rights of self-determination"; attending physician authorized to remove treatment after finding that patient is in a terminal condition, obtaining consent of family, and considering expressed wishes of patient).[6]

As these cases demonstrate, the common-law doctrine of informed consent is viewed as generally encompassing the right of a competent individual to refuse medical treatment. Beyond that, these decisions demonstrate both similarity and diversity in their approach to decision of what all agree is a perplexing question with unusually strong moral and ethical overtones. State courts have available to them for decision a number of sources - state constitutions, statutes, and common law - which are not available to us. In this Court, the question is simply and starkly whether the United States Constitution prohibits Missouri from choosing the rule of decision which it did. This is the first case in which we have been squarely presented with the issue of whether the United States Constitution grants what is in common parlance referred to as a "right to die." We follow the judicious counsel of our decision in Twin City Bank v. Nebeker, 167 U.S. 196, 202 (1897), where we said that in deciding "a question of such magnitude and importance ... it is the [better] part of wisdom not to attempt, by any general statement, to cover every possible phase of the subject."

The Fourteenth Amendment provides that no State shall "deprive any person of life, liberty, or property, without due process of law." The principle that a competent person has a constitutionally protected liberty interest in refusing unwanted medical treatment may be inferred from our prior decisions. In Jacobson v. Massachusetts, 197 U.S. 11, 24-30 (1905), for instance, the Court balanced an individual's liberty interest in declining an unwanted small pox vaccine against the State's interest in preventing disease. Decisions prior to the incorporation of the Fourth Amendment into the Fourteenth Amendment analyzed searches and seizures involving the body under the Due Process Clause and were thought to implicate substantial liberty interests. See, e.g., Breithaupt v. Abrams, 352 U.S. 432, 439 (1957) ("As against the right of an individual that his person be held inviolable ... must be set the interests of society ...").

Just this Term, in the course of holding that a state's procedures for administering antipsychotic medication to prisoners were sufficient to satisfy due process concerns, we recognized that prisoners possess "a significant liberty interest in avoiding the unwanted administration of antipsychotic drugs under the Due Process Clause of the Fourteenth Amendment." Washington v. Harper _____ U.S. _____, _____ (1990) (slip op., at 9); see also Id., at _____ (slip op., at 17) ("The forcible injection of medication into a nonconsenting person's body represents a substantial interference with that person's liberty"). Still other cases support the recognition of a general liberty interests); Parham v. J.R., 442 U.S. 584, 600 (1979) ("a child, in common with adults, has a substantial liberty interest in not being confined unnecessarily for medical treatment").

But determining that a person has a "liberty interest" under the Due Process Clause does not end the inquiry;[7] "whether respondent's constitutional rights have been violated must be determined by balancing his liberty interests against the relevant state interests." Youngberg v. Romeo, 457 U.S. 307, 321 (1982). See also Mills v. Rogers, 457 U.S. 291, 299 (1982).

Petitioners insist that under the general holdings of our cases, the forced administration of life-sustaining medical treatment, and even of artificially-delivered food and water essential to life, would implicate a competent person's liberty interest. Although we think the logic of the cases discussed above would embrace such a liberty interest, the dramatic consequences involved in refusal of such treatment would inform the inquiry as to whether the deprivation of that interest is constitutionally permissible. But for purposes of this case, we assume that the United States Constitution would grant a competent person a constitutionally protected right to refuse lifesaving hydration and nutrition.

Petitioners go on to assert that an incompetent person should possess the same right in this respect as is possessed by a competent person. They rely primarily on our decisions in Parham v. J.R., supra, and Youngberg v. Romeo, 457 U.S. 307 (1982). In Parham, we held that a mentally disturbed minor child had a liberty interest in "not being confined unnecessarily of medical treatment," 442 U.S., at 600, but we certainly did not intimate that such a minor child, after commitment, would have a liberty interest in refusing treatment, In Youngberg, we held that a seriously retarded adult had a liberty interest in safety and freedom from bodily restraint, 457 U.S., at 320. Youngberg, however, did not deal with decisions to administer or withhold medical treatment.

The difficulty with petitioners' claim is that in a sense it begs the question: an incompetent person is not able to make an informed and voluntary choice to exercise a hypothetical right to refuse treatment or any other right. Such a "right" must be exercised for her, if at all, by some sort of surrogate. Here, Missouri has in effect recognized that under certain circumstances a surrogate may act for the patient in electing to have hydration and nutrition withdrawn in such a way as to cause death, but it has established a procedural safeguard to assure that the action of the surrogate conforms as best it may to the wishes expressed by the patient while competent. Missouri requires that evidence of the incompetent's wishes as to the withdrawal of treatment be proved by clear and convincing evidence. The question, then, is whether the United States Constitution forbids the establishment of this procedural requirement by the State. We hold that it does not.

Whether or not Missouri's clear and convincing evidence requirement comports with the United States Constitution depends in part on what interests the State may properly seek to protect in this situation. Missouri relies on its interest in the protection and preservation of human life, and there can be no gainsaying this interest. As a general matter, the States - indeed, all civilized nations - demonstrate their commitment to life by treating homicide as serious crime. Moreover, the majority of States in this country have laws imposing criminal penalties on one who assists another to commit suicide.[8] We do not think a State is required to remain neutral in the face of an informed and voluntary decision by a physically-able adult to starve to death.

But in the context presented here, a State has more particular interests at stake. The choice between life and death is a deeply personal decision of obvious and overwhelming finality. We believe Missouri may legitimately seek to safeguard the personal element of this choice through the imposition of heightened evidentiary requirements. It cannot be disputed that the Due Process Clause protects an interest in life as well as an interest in refusing life-sustaining medical treatment. Not all incompetent patients will have loved ones available to serve as surrogate decisionmakers. And even where family members are present, "[t]here will, of course, be some unfortunate situations in which family members will not act to protect a patient." In re Jobes, 108 N.J. 394, 419, 529 A. 2d 434, 477 (1987). A State is entitled to guard against potential abuses in such situation. Similarly, a State is entitled to consider that a judicial proceeding to make a determination regarding an incompetent's wishes may very well not be an adversarial one, with the added guarantee of accurate factfinding that the adversary process brings with it.[9] See Ohio v. Akron Center for Reproductive Health, ____ U.S. ____, ____ (1990) (slip op. at 10-11). Finally, we think a State may properly decline to make judgments about the "quality" of life that a particular individual may enjoy, and simply assert an unqualified interest in the preservation of human life to be weighed against the constitutionally protected interests of the individual.

In our view, Missouri has permissibly sought to advance these interests through the adoption of a "clear and convincing" standard of proof to govern such proceedings. "The function of a standard of proof, as that concept is embodied in the Due Process Clause and in the realm of factfinding, is to `instruct the factfinder concerning the degree of confidence our society thinks he should have in the correctness of factual conclusions for a particular type of adjudication.'" Addington v. Texas, 441 U.S. 418, 423 (1979) (quoting In re Winship, 397 U.S. 358, 370 (1970) (Harlan, J., concurring)). "This Court has mandated an intermediate standard of proof - `clear and convincing evidence' - when the individual interests at stake in a state proceeding are both `particularly important' and `more substantial than mere loss of money.'" Santosky v. Kramer, 455 U.S. 745, 756 (1982) (quoting Addington, supra, at 424). Thus, such a standard has been required in deportation proceedings, Woodby v. INS, 385 U.S. 276 (1966), in denaturalization proceedings, Schneiderman v. United States, 320 U.S. 118 (1943), in civil commitment proceedings, Addington, supra, and in proceedings for the termination of parental rights. Santosky, supra,[10] Further, this level of proof, "or an even higher one, has traditionally been imposed in cases involving allegations of civil fraud, and in a variety of other kinds of civil cases involving such issues as ... lost wills, oral contracts to make bequests, and the like." Woodby, supra, at 285, n. 18.

We think it self-evident that the interests at stake in the instant proceedings are more substantial, both on an individual and societal level, than those involved in a run-of-the-mine civil dispute. But not only does the standard of proof reflect the importance of a particular adjudication, it also serves as "a societal judgment about how the risk of error should be distributed between the litigants." Santosky, supra, 455 U.S. at 755; Addington, supra, at 423. The more stringent the burden of proof a party must bear, the more that party bears the risk of an erroneous decision. we believe that Missouri may permissibly place an increased risk of an erroneous decision on those seeking to terminate an incompetent individual's life-sustaining treatment. An erroneous decision not to terminate results in a maintenance of the status quo; the possibility of subsequent developments such as advancements in medical science, the discovery of new evidence regarding the patient's intent, changes in the law, or simply the unexpected death of the patient despite the administration of life-sustaining treatment, at least create the potential that a wrong decision will eventually be corrected or its impact mitigated. An erroneous decision to withdraw life-sustaining treatment, however, is not susceptible of correction. In Santosky, one of the factors which led the Court to require proof by clear and convincing evidence in a proceeding to terminate parental rights was that a decision in such a case was final and irrevocable. Santosky, supra, at 759. The same must surely be said of the decision to discontinue hydration and nutrition of a patient such as Nancy Cruzan, which all agree will result in her death.

It is also worth noting that most, if not all, States simply forbid oral testimony entirely in determining the wishes of parties in transactions which, while important, simply do not have the consequences that a decision to terminate a person's life does. At common law and by statute in most States, the parole evidence rule prevents the variations of the terms of a written contract by oral testimony. The statute of frauds makes unenforceable oral contracts to leave property by will, and statutes regulating the making of wills universally require that those instruments be in writing. See 2 A. Corbin, Contracts Section 398, pp. 360-361 (1950); 2 W. Page, Law of Wills Sections 19.3-19.5, pp. 61-71 (1960). There is no doubt that statutes requiring wills to be in writing, and statutes of frauds which require that a contract to make a will be in writing, on occasion frustrate the effectuation of the intent of a particular decedent, just as Missouri's requirement of proof in this case may have frustrated the effectuation of the notfully-expressed desires of Nancy Cruzan. But the Constitution does not require general rules to work faultlessly; no general rule can.

In sum, we conclude that a State may apply a clear and convincing evidence standard in proceedings where a guardian seeks to discontinue nutrition and hydration of a person diagnosed to be in a persistent vegetative state. We note that many courts which have adopted some sort of substituted judgment procedure in situations like this, whether they limit consideration of evidence to the prior expressed wishes of the incompetent individual, or whether they allow more general proof of what the individual's decision would have been, require a clear and convincing standard of proof for such evidence. See, e.g., Longeway, 133 Ill, 2d, at 50-51, 549 N.E. 2d at 300; McConnell, 209 Conn., at 707-710, 553 A. 2d at 604-605; O'Connor, 72 N.Y. 2d, at 529-530, 531 N.E. 2d, at 613; In re Gardner, 534 A. 2d 947, 952-953 (Me. 1987); In re Jobes, 108 N.J., at 412-413, 529 A. 2d, at 443; Leach v. Akron

General Medical Center, 68 Ohio Misc. 1, 11, 426 N.E. 2d 809, 815 (1980).

The Supreme Court of Missouri held that in this case the testimony adduced at trial did not amount to clear and convincing proof of the patient's desire to have hydration and nutrition withdrawn. In so doing, it reversed a decision of the Missouri trial court which had found that the evidence "suggest[ed]" Nancy Cruzan would not have desired to continue such measure, App. to Pet. for Cert. A98, but which had not adopted the standard of "clear and convincing evidence" enunciated by the Supreme Court. The testimony adduced at trial consisted primarily of Nancy Cruzan's statements made to a housemate about a year before her accident that she would not want to live should she face life as a "vegetable," and other observations to the same effect. The observations did not deal in terms with withdrawal of medical treatment or of hydration and nutrition. We cannot say that the Supreme Court of Missouri committed constitutional error in reaching the conclusion that it did.[11]

Petitioners alternatively contend that Missouri must accept the "substituted judgment" of close family members even in the absence of substantial proof that their views reflect the views of the patient. They rely primarily upon our decisions in Michael H. v. Gerald D., 491 U.S. ____ (1989), and Parham v. J.R., 442 U.S. 584 (1979). But we do not think these cases support their claim. In Michael H., we upheld the constitutionality of California's favored treatment of traditional family relationships; such a holding may not be turned around into a constitutional requirement that a State must recognize the primacy of those relationships in a situation like this. And in Parham, where the patient was a minor, we also upheld the constitutionality of a state scheme in which parents made certain decisions for mentally ill minors. Here again petitioners would seek to turn a decision which allowed a State to rely on family decisionmaking into a constitutional requirement that the State recognize such decisionmaking. But constitutional law does not work that way.

No doubt is engendered by anything in this record but that Nancy Cruzan's mother and father are loving and caring parents. If the State were required by the United States Constitution to repose a right of "substituted judgment" with anyone, the Cruzans would surely qualify. But we do not think the Due Process Clause requires the State to repose judgment on these matter with anyone but the patient herself. Close family members may have a strong feeling - a feeling not at all ignoble or unworthy, but not entirely disinterested, either - that they do not wish to witness the continuation of the life of a loved one which they regard as hopeless, meaningless, and even degrading. But there is no automatic assurance that the view of close family members will necessarily be the same as the patient's would have been had she been confronted with the prospect of her situation while competent. All of the reasons previously discussed for allowing Missouri to require clear and convincing evidence of the patient's wishes lead us to conclude that the State may choose to defer only to those wishes, rather than confide the decision to close family members.[12]

The judgment of the Supreme Court of Missouri is   Affirmed.

JUSTICE O'CONNOR, concurring.

I agree that a protected liberty interest in refusing unwanted medical treatment may be inferred from our prior decisions, see ante at 13, and that the refusal of artificially delivered food and water is encompassed within that liberty interest. See ante, at 15. I write separately to clarify why I believe this to be so.

As the Court notes, the liberty interest in refusing medical treatment flows from decisions involving the State's invasions into the body. see ante, at 14. Because our notions of liberty are inextricably entwined with our idea of physical freedom and self-determination, the Court has often deemed state incursions into the body repugnant to the interests protected by the Due Process clause. See e.g., Rochin v. California, 342 U.S. 165, 172 (1952) ("Illegally breaking into the privacy of the petitioner, the struggle to open his mouth and remove what was there, the forcible extraction of his stomach's contents ... is bound to offend even hardened sensibilities"); Union Pacific R. Co. v. Botsford, 141 U.S. 250, 251 (1891). Our Fourth Amendment jurisprudence has echoed this same concern. See Schmerber v. California, 384 U.S. 757,772 (1966) ("The integrity of an individual's person is a cherished value of our society"); Winston v. Lee, 470 U.S. 753, 759 (1985) ("A compelled surgical intrusion into an individual's body for evidence ... implicates expectations of privacy and security of such magnitude that the intrusion may be 'unreasonable' even if likely to produce evidence of a crime"). The State's imposition of medical treatment on an unwilling competent adult necessarily involves some form of restraint and intrusion. A seriously ill or dying patient whose wishes are not honored may feel a captive of the machinery required for life-sustaining measure or other medical interventions. Such forced treatment may burden that individual's liberty interests as much as any state coercion. See, e.g. Washington v. Harper, 494 U.S. ____, ____ (1990); Parham v. J.R., 442 U.S. 584, 600 (1979) ("It is not disputed that a child, in common with adults, has a substantial liberty interest in not being confined unnecessarily for medical treatment").

The State's artificial provision of nutrition and hydration implicates identical concerns. Artificial feeding cannot readily be distinguished from other forms of medical treatment. See e.g., Council on Ethical and Judicial Affairs, American Medical Association, AMA Ethical Opinion 2.20, Withholding or Withdrawing Life-Prolonging Medical Treatment current Opinions 13 (1989); The Hastings Center, Guidelines on the Termination of Life-Sustaining Treatment and the Care of the Dying 59 (1987). Whether or not the techniques used to pass food and water into the patient's alimentary tract are termed "medical treatment," it is clear they all involve some degree of intrusion and restraint. Feeding a patient by means of a nasogastric tube requires a physician to pass a long flexible tube through the patient's nose, throat and esophagus and into the stomach. Because of the discomfort such a tube cause, "[m]any patients need to be restrained forcibly and their hands put into large mittens to prevent them from removing the tube." Major, The Medical Procedures for Providing Food and Water: Indications and Effects, in By No Extraordinary Means: The Choice to

Forgo Life-Sustaining Food and Water 25 (J. Lynn ed. 1986). A gastrostomy tube (as was used to provide food and water to Nancy Cruzan, see ante, at 2) or jejunostomy tube must be surgically implanted into the stomach or small intestine. Office of Technology Assessment Task Force, Life-Sustaining Technologies and the Elderly 282 (1988). Requiring a competent adult to endure such procedures against her will burdens the patient's liberty, dignity, and freedom to determine the course of her own treatment. Accordingly, the liberty guaranteed by the Due Process Clause must protect, it it protects anything, an individual's deeply personal decision to reject medical treatment, including the artificial delivery of food and water.

I also write separately to emphasize that the Court does not today decide the issue whether a State must also give effect to the decisions of a surrogate decisionmaker. See ante, at 22, n. 13. In my view, such a duty may well be constitutionally required to protect the patient's liberty interest in refusing medical treatment. Few individuals provide explicit oral or written instructions regarding their intent to refuse medical treatment should they become incompetent.[1] States which decline to consider any evidence other than such instructions may frequently fail to honor a patient's intent. Such failures might be avoided if the State considered an equally probative source of evidence: the patient's appointment of a proxy to make health care decisions on her behalf. Delegating the authority to make medical decisions to a family member or friend is becoming a common method of planning for the future. See, e.g., Areen, The Legal Status of Consent Obtained from Families of Adult Patients to Withhold or Withdraw Treatment, 258 JAMA 229, 230 (1987). Several States have recognized the practical wisdom of such a procedure by enacting durable power of attorney statutes that specifically authorize an individual to appoint a surrogate to make medical treatment decisions.[2] Some state courts have suggested that an agent appointed pursuant to a general durable power of attorney statute would also be empowered to make health care decisions on behalf of the patient.[3] See e.g., In re Peter, 108 N.J. 365, 378-379, 529 A. 2d 419, 426 (1987); see also 73 Op. Md. Atty. Gen. No. 88-0046 (1988) (interpreting Md. Est. & Trusts Code Ann. Sections 13-601 to 13-602 (1974), as authorizing a delegatee to make health care decision). Other States allow an individual to designate a proxy to carry out the intent of a living will.[4] These procedures for surrogate decisionmaking, which appear to be rapidly gaining in acceptance, may be a valuable additional safeguard of the patient's interest in directing his medical care. Moreover, as patients are likely to select a family member as a surrogate, see 2 President's Commission for the Study of Ethical Problems in Medicine and Biomedical and Behavioral Research, Making Health care Decision 240 (1982), giving effect to a proxy's decisions may also protect the "freedom of personal choice in matters of ... family life." Cleveland Board of Education v. LaFleur, 414 U.S. 632, 639 (1974).

Today's decision, holding only that the Constitution permits a State to require clear and convincing evidence of Nancy Cruzan's desire to have artificial hydration and nutrition withdrawn, does not preclude a future determination that the Constitution requires the States to implement the decisions of a patient's duly appointed surrogate. Nor does it prevent States from developing other approaches for protecting an incompetent individual's liberty interest in refusing medical treatment. As is evident from the Court's survey of state court decisions, see ante at 6-13, no national consensus has yet emerged on the best solution for this difficult and sensitive problem. Today we decide only that one State's practice does not violate the Constitution; the more challenging task of crafting appropriate procedures for safeguarding incompetents' liberty interests is entrusted to the "laboratory" of the States, New State Ice Co. v. Liebmann, 285 U.S. 262, 311 (1932) (Brandeis, J., dissenting), in the first instance.

JUSTICE SCALIA, concurring.

The various opinions in this case portray quite clearly the difficult, indeed agonizing, questions that are presented by the constantly increasing power of science to keep the human body alive for longer than any reasonable person would want to inhabit it. The States have begun to grapple with these problems through legislation. I am concerned, from the tenor of today's opinions, that we are poised to confuse that enterprise as successfully as we have confused the enterprise of legislating concerning abortion - requiring it to be conducted against a background of federal constitutional imperatives that are unknown because they are being newly crafted from Term to Term. That would be a great misfortune.

While I agree with the Court's analysis today, and therefore join in its opinion, I would have preferred that we announce, clearly and promptly, that the federal courts have no business in this field; that American law has always accorded the State the power to prevent, by force if necessary, suicide - including suicide by refusing to take appropriate measures necessary to preserve one's life; that the point at which life becomes "worthless," and the point at which the means necessary to preserve it become "extraordinary" or "inappropriate," are neither set forth in the Constitution nor known to the nine Justices of this Court any better than they are known to nine people picked at random from the Kansas City telephone directory; and hence, that even when it is demonstrated by clear and convincing evidence that a patient no longer wishes certain measures to be taken to preserve her life, it is up to the citizens of Missouri to decide, through their elected representatives, whether that wish will be honored. It is quite impossible (because the Constitution says nothing about the matter) that those citizens will decide upon a line less lawful than the one we would choose; and it is unlikely (because we know no more about "life-and-death" than they do, that they will decide upon a line less reasonable.

The test of the Due Process Clause does not protect individuals against deprivations of liberty simpliciter. It protects them against deprivations of liberty "without due process of law." To determine that such a deprivation would not occur if Nancy Cruzan were forced to take nourishment against her will, it is unnecessary to reopen the historically recurrent debate over whether "due process" includes substantive restrictions. Compare Murray's Lessee v. Hoboken Land and Improvement Co., 18 How. 272 (1856), with Scott v. Sandford, 19 How.

393, 450 (1857); compare <u>Tyson & Bro. v. United Theatre Ticket Office, Inc.</u>, 273 U.S. 418 (1927), with <u>Olsen v. Nebraska ex re. Western Reference & Bond Assn., Inc.</u>, 313 U.S. 236, 246-247 (1941); compare <u>Ferguson v. Skrupa</u>, 372 U.S. 726, 730 (1963), with <u>Moore v. East Cleveland</u>, 431 U.S. 494 (1977) (plurality opinion); <u>see</u> Easterbrook, Substance and Due Process, 1982 S. Ct. Rev. 85; Monaghan, Our Perfect Constitution, 56 N.Y.U.L. Rev. 353 (1981). It is at least true that no "substantive due process" claim can be maintained unless the claimant demonstrates that the State has deprived him of a right historically and traditionally protected against State interference. <u>Michael H. v. Gerald D.</u>, 491 U.S. ____, ____ (1989) (plurality opinion); <u>Bowers v. Hardwick</u>, 478 U.S. 186, 192 (1986); <u>Moore</u>, <u>supra</u>, at 502-503 (plurality opinion). That cannot possibly be established here.

At common law in England, a suicide - defined as one who "deliberately puts an end to his own existence, or commits any unlawful malicious act, the consequence of which is his own death," 4 W. Blackstone, Commentaries *189 - was criminally liable. <u>Ibid</u>. Although the States abolished the penalties imposed by the common law (<u>i.e.</u>, forfeiture and ignominious burial), they did so to spare the innocent family, and not to legitimize the act. case law at the time of the Fourteenth Amendment generally held that assisting suicide was a criminal offense. <u>See</u> Marzen, O'Dowd, Crone, & Balch, Suicide: A Constitutional Right?, 24 Duquesne L. Rev. 1, 76 (1985) ("In short, twenty-one of the thirty-seven states, and eighteen of the thirty ratifying states prohibited assisting suicide. Only eight of the states, and seven of the ratifying states, definitely did not"); <u>see also</u> 1 F. Wharton, Criminal Law Section 122 (6th rev. ed. 1868). The System of Penal Law presented to the House of Representatives by Representative Livingston in 1828 would have criminalized assisted suicide. E. Livingston, A System of Penal Law, Penal Code 122 (1828). The Field Penal Code, adopted by the Dakota Territory in 1877, proscribed attempted suicide and assisted suicide. Marzen, O'Dowd, Crone, & Balch, 24 Duquesne L. Rev., at 76-77. And most States that did not explicitly prohibit assisted suicide in 1868 recognized, when the issue arose in the 50 years following the Fourteenth Amendment's ratification, that assisted and (in some cases) attempted suicide were unlawful. <u>Id.</u>, at 77-100; 148-242 (surveying development of States' laws). Thus, "there is no significant support for the claim that a right to suicide is so rooted in our tradition that it may be deemed `fundamental' or `implicit in the concept of ordered liberty.'" <u>Id.</u>, at 100 (quoting <u>Palko v. Connecticut</u>, 302 U.S. 319, 325 (1937)).

Petitioners rely on three distinctions to separate Nancy Cruzan's case from ordinary suicide: (1) that she is permanently incapacited and in pain; (2) that she would bring on her death not by any affirmative act buy by merely declining treatment that provides nourishment; and (3) that preventing her from effectuating her presumed wish to die requires violation of her bodily integrity. None of these suffices. Suicide was not excused even when committed "to avoid those ills which [persons] had not the fortitude to endure." 4 Blackstone, <u>supra</u>, at *189. "The life of those to whom life has become a burden - of those who are hopelessly diseased or fatally wounded - nay, even the lives of criminals condemned to death, are under the protection of the law, equally as the lives of those who are in the full tide of life's enjoyment, and anxious to continue to live." Blackburn v. State, 23 Ohio St. 146, 163 (1873). Thus, a man who prepared a poison, and placed it within reach of his wife, "to put an end to her suffering" from a terminal illness was convicted of murder, People v. Roberts, 211 Mich. 187, 198 N. W. 690, 693 (1920); the "incurable suffering of the suicide, as a legal question, could hardly affect the degree of criminality ... ." Note, 30 Yale L.J. 408, 412 (1921) (discussing Roberts). Nor would the imminence of the patient's death have affected liability. "The lives of all are equally under the protection of the law, and under that protection to their last moment. ... [Assisted suicide] is declared by the law to be murder, irrespective of the wishes or the condition of the party to whom the poison is administered. ..." Blackburn, supra, at 163; see also Commonwealth v. Bowen, 13 Mass. 356, 360 (1816).

The second asserted distinction - suggested by the recent cases canvassed by the Court concerning the right to refuse treatment, ante, at 5-12 - relies on the dichotomy between action and inaction. Suicide, it is said, consists of an affirmative act to end one's life; refusing treatment is not an affirmative act "causing" death, but merely a passive acceptance of the natural process of dying. I readily acknowledge that the distinction between action and inaction has some bearing upon the legislative judgment of what ought to be prevented as suicide - though even there it would seem to me unreasonable to draw the line precisely between action and inaction, rather than between various forms of inaction. It would not make much sense to say that one may not kill oneself by walking into the sea, but may sit on the beach until submerged by the incoming tide; or that one may not intentionally lock oneself into a cold storage locker, but may refrain from coming indoors when the temperature drops below freezing. Even as a legislative matter, in other words, the intelligent line does not fall between action and inaction but between those forms of inaction that consist of abstaining from "ordinary" care and those that consist of abstaining from "excessive" or "heroic" measures. Unlike action vs. inaction, that is not a line to be discerned by logic or legal analysis, and we should not pretend that it is.

But to return to the principal point from present purposes: the irrelevance of the action-inaction distinction. Starving oneself to death is no different from putting a gun to one's temple as far as the commmon-law definition of suicide is concerned; the cause of death in both cases is the suicide's conscious decision to "pu[t] an end to his own existence." 4 Blackstone, supra, at *189. See In re Caulk, 125 N.J. 226, 232, 480 A. 2d 93, 97 (1984); State ex rel. White v. Narick, ___ W.Va. ___, 292 S.E. 2d 54 (1982); Von Holden v. Chapman, 87 App. Div. 2d 66, 450 N.Y.S. 2d 623 (1982). Of course the common law rejected the action-inaction distinction in other contexts involving the taking of human life as well. In the prosecution of a parent for the starvation death of her infant, it was no defense that the infant's death was "caused" by no action of the parent but by the natural process of starvation, or by the infant's natural inability to provide for itself. See Lewis v. State, 72 Ga. 164 (1883); People v. McDonald, 49 Hun 67, 1 N.Y.S. 703 (1888); Commonwealth v. Hall, 322 Mass. 523,

528, 78 N.E. 2d 644, 647 (1948) (collecting cases); F. Wharton, Law of Homicide Sections 134-135, 304 (2d ed. 1875); 2 J. Bishop, Commentaries on the Criminal Law Section 686 (5th ed. 1872); J. Hawley & M. McGregor, Criminal Law 152 (3rd ed. 1899). A physician, moreover, could be criminally liable for failure to provide care that could have extended the patient's life, even if death was immediately caused by the underlying disease that the physician failed to treat. Barrow v. State, 17 Okla. Cr. 340, 188 P. 351 (1920); People v. Phillips, 64 Cal. 2d 574, 414 P. 2d 353 (1966).

It is not surprising, therefore, that the early cases considering the claimed right to refuse medical treatment dismissed as specious the nice distinction between "passively submitting to death and actively seeking it. The distinction may be merely verbal, as it would be if an adult sought death by starvation instead of a drug. If the State may interrupt one mode of self-destruction, it may with equal authority interfere with the other." John F. Kennedy Memorial Hosp. v. Heston, 58 N.J. 576, 581-582, 279 A. 2d 670, 672-673 (1971); see also Application of President & Directors of Georgetown College, Inc., 118 U.S. App. D.C. 80,88-89, 331 F. 2d 1000, 1008-1009 (Wright, J., in chambers), cert. denied, 377 U.S. 978 (1964).

The third asserted basis of distinction - that frustrating Nancy Cruzan's wish to die in the present case requires interference with her bodily integrity - is likewise inadequate, because such interference is impermissible only if one begs the question whether her refusal to undergo the treatment on her own is suicide. It has always been lawful not only for the State, but even for private citizens, to interfere with bodily integrity to prevent a felony. See Phillips v. Trull, 11 Johns. 486 (N.Y. 1814); City Council v. Payne, 2 Nott & McCord 475 (S.C. 1821); Vandeveer v. Mattocks, 3 Ind. 479 (1852); T. Cooley, Law of Torts 174-175 (1879); Wilgus, Arrest Without a Warrant, 22 Mich. L. Rev. 673 (1924); Restatement of Torts Section 119 (1934). That general rule has of course been applied to suicide. At common law, even a private person's use of force to prevent suicide was privileged. Colby v. Jackson, 12 N.H. 526, 530-531 (1842); Look v. Choate, 108 Mass. 116, 120 (1871); Commonwealth v. Mink, 123 Mass. 422, 429 (1877); In re Doyle, 15 R.I. 537, 539, 18 A. 159, 159-160 (1889); Porter v. Ritch, 70 Conn. 235, 255, 39 A. 169, 175 (1898); State v. Hembd, 305 Minn. 120, 130, 232 N.W. 2d 872, 878 (1975); 2 C. Addison, Law of Torts Section 819 (1876); Cooley, supra, at 179-180. It is not even reasonable, much less required by the Constitution, to maintain that although the State has the right to prevent a person from slashing his wrists it does not have the power to apply physical force to prevent him from doing so, nor the power, should he succeed, to apply, coercively if necessary, medical measures to stop the flow of blood. The state-run hospital, I am certain, is not liable under 42 U.S.C. Section 1983 for violation of constitutional rights, nor the private hospital liable under general tort law, if, in a State where suicide is unlawful, it pumps out the stomach of a person who has intentionally taken an overdose of barbiturates, despite that person's wishes to the contrary.

The dissents of JUSTICES BRENNAN and STEVENS make a plausible case for our intervention here only by embracing - the latter explicitly and the former by implication - a political principle that the States are

35

free to adopt, but that is demonstrably not imposed by the Constitution. "The State," says JUSTICE BRENNAN, "has no legitimate general interest in someone's life, completely abstracted from the interest of the person living that life, that could outweigh the person's choice <u>to avoid medical treatment</u>." <u>Post</u>, at 14 (emphasis added). The italicized phrase sounds moderate enough, and is all that is needed to cover the present case - but the proposition cannot <u>logically</u> be so limited. One who accepts if must also accept, I think, that the State has no such legitimate interest that could outweigh "the person's choice <u>to put an end to her life</u>." Similarly, if one agrees with JUSTICE BRENNAN that "the State's general interest in life must accede to Nancy Cruzan's particularized and intense interest in self-determination <u>in her choice of medical treatment</u>, <u>ibid</u>. (emphasis added), he must also believe that the State must accede to her "particularized and intense interest in self-determination <u>in her choice whether to continue living or to die</u>." For insofar as balancing the relative interests of the State and the individual is concerned, there is nothing distinctive about accepting death through the refusal of "medical treatment," as opposed to accepting it through the refusal of food, or through the failure to shut off the engine and get out of the car after parking in one's garage after work. Suppose that Nancy Cruzan were in precisely the condition she is in today, except that she could be fed and digest food and water, <u>without</u> artificial assistance. How is the State's "interest" in keeping her alive thereby increased, or her interest in deciding whether she wants to continue living reduced? It seems to me, in other words, that JUSTICE BRENNAN'S position ultimately rests upon the proposition that it is none of the State's business if a person wants to commit suicide. JUSTICE STEVENS is explicit on the point; "Choices about death touch the core of liberty ... . [N]ot much may be said with confidence about death unless it is said from faith, and that alone is reason enough to protect the freedom to conform choices about death to individual conscience." <u>Post</u>, at 13-14. This is a view that some societies have held, and that our States are free to adopt if they wish. But it is not a view imposed by our constitutional traditions, in which the power of the State to prohibit suicide is unquestionable.

What I have said above is not meant to suggest that I would think it desirable, if we were sure that Nancy Cruzan wanted to die, to keep her alive by the means at issue here. I assert only that the Constitution has nothing to say about the subject. To raise up a constitutional right here we would have to create out of nothing (for it exists neither in text nor tradition) some constitutional principle whereby, although the State may insist that an individual come in out of the cold and eat food, it may not insist that he take medicine; and although it may pump his stomach empty of poison he has ingested, it may not fill his stomach with food he has failed to ingest. Are there, then, no reasonable and humane limits that ought not to be exceeded in requiring an individual to preserve his own life? There obviously are, but they are not set forth in the Due Process Clause. What assures us that those limits will not be exceeded is the same constitutional guarantee that is the source of most of our protection - what protects us, for example, from being assessed a tax of 100% of our income above the subsistence level, from being forbidden to drive cars, or from being required to send our children to school for 10 hours a day, none of which horribles is categorically prohibited by the Constitution. Our salvation is the Equal Protection Clause, which requires the democratic majority to accept for themselves and their loved ones what they impose on you and me. This Court need not, and has no authority to, inject itself into every field of human activity where irrationality and oppression may theoretically occur, and if it tries to do so it will destroy itself.

JUSTICE BRENNAN, with whom JUSTICE MARSHALL and JUSTICE BLACKMUN join, dissenting.

"Medical technology has effectively created a twilight zone of suspended animation where death commences while life, in some form continues. Some patients, however, want no part of a life sustained only be medical technology. Instead, they prefer a plan of medical treatment that allows nature to take its course and permits them to die with dignity."[1]

Nancy Cruzan has dwelt in that twilight zone for six years. She is oblivious to her surroundings and will remain so. Cruzan v. Harmon, 760 S.W. 2d 408, 411 (Mo. 1988). Her body twitches only reflexively, without consciousness. Ibid. The areas of her brain that once thought, felt, and experienced sensations have degenerated badly and are continuing to do so. The cavities remaining are filling with cerebrospinal fluid. The "`cerebral cortical atrophy is irreversible, permanent, progressive and ongoing.'" Ibid. "Nancy will never interact meaningfully with her environment again. She will remain in a persistent vegetative state until her death." Id., at 422.2 Because she cannot swallow, her nutrition and hydration are delivered through a tube surgically implanted in her stomach.

A grown woman at the time of the accident, Nancy had previously expressed her wish to forgo continuing medical care under circumstances such as these. Her family and her friends are convinced that this is what she would want. See n. 20, infra. A guardian ad litem appointed by the trial court is also convinced that this is what Nancy would want. See 760 S.W. 2d, at 444 (Higgins, J., dissenting from denial of rehearing). Yet the Missouri Supreme Court, alone among state courts deciding such a question, has determined that an irreversibly vegetative patient will remain a passive prisoner of medical technology - for Nancy, perhaps for the next 30 years. See id., at 424, 427,

Today the Court, while tentatively accepting that there is some degree of constitutionally protected liberty interest in avoiding unwanted medical treatment, including life-sustaining medical treatment such as artificial nutrition and hydration, affirms the decision of the Missouri Supreme Court. The majority opinion, as I read it, would affirm that decision on the ground that a State may require "clear and convincing" evidence of Nancy Cruzan's prior decision to forgo life-sustaining treatment under circumstances such as hers in order to ensure that her actual wishes are honored. See ante, at 17-19, 22. Because I believe that Nancy Cruzan has a fundamental right to be free of unwanted artificial nutrition and hydration, which right is not outweighed by any interests of the State, and because I find that the improperly biased procedural obstacles imposed by the Missouri Supreme Court impermissibly burden that right, I respectfully dissent. Nancy Cruzan is entitled to choose to die with dignity.

I

A

"[T]he timing of death - once a matter of fate - is now a matter of human choice." Office of Technology Assessment Task Force, Life Sustaining Technologies and the Elderly 41 (1988). Of the approximately two million people who die each year, 80% die in hospitals and long-term care institutions,3 and perhaps 70% of those after a decision to forgo life-sustaining treatment has been made.4. Nearly every death involves a decision whether to undertake some medical procedure that could prolong the process of dying. Such decisions are difficult and personal. They must be made on the basis of individual values, informed by medical realities, yet within a framework governed by law. The role of the court is confined to defining that framework, delineating the ways in which government may and may not participate in such decisions.

The question before this Court is a relatively narrow one" whether the Due Process Clause allows Missouri to require a now-incompetent patient in an irreversible persistent vegetative state to remain on life-support absent rigorously clear and convincing evidence that avoiding the treatment represents the patient's prior, express choice. See ante, at 13. If a fundamental right is at issue, Missouri's rule of decision must be scrutinized under the standards this Court has always applied in such circumstances. As we said in Zablocki v. Redhail, 434 U.S. 372, 388 (1978), if a requirement imposed by a State "significantly interferes with the exercise of a fundamental right, it cannot be upheld unless it is supported by sufficiently important state interests and is closely tailored to effectuate only those interests." The Constitution imposes on this Court the obligation to "examine carefully ... the extent to which[the legitimate government interests advanced] are served by the challenged regulation." Moore v. East Cleveland, 431 U.S. 494, 499 (1977). See also Carey v. Population Services International, 431 U.S. 678, 690 (1977) (invalidating a requirement that bore "no relation to the State's interest"). An evidentiary rule, just as a substantive prohibition, must meet these standards if it significantly burdens a fundamental liberty interest. Fundamental rights "are protected not only against heavy-handed frontal attack, but also from being stifled by more subtle governmental interference." Bates v. Little Rock, 361 U.S. 516, 523, (1960).

B

The starting point for our legal analysis must be whether a competent person has a constitutional right to avoid unwanted medical care. Earlier this Term, this Court held that the Due Process Clause of the Fourteenth Amendment confers a significant liberty interest in avoiding unwanted medical treatment. Washington v. Harper, 494 U.S. _____, _____ (1990). Today, the Court concedes that our prior decisions "support the recognition of a general liberty interest in refusing medical treatment." See ante, at 14. The Court, however, avoids discussing either the measure of that liberty interest or its application by assuming, for purposes of this case only, that a competent person has a constitutionally protected liberty interest in being free of unwanted artificial nutrition and hydration. See ante, at 15. JUSTICE O'CONNOR'S opinion is less parsimonious. She openly affirms that "the Court has often deemed state incursions into the body repugnant to the interests protected by the Due Process Clause," that there is a liberty interest in avoiding unwanted medical treatment and that it encompasses the right to be free of "artificially delivered food and water." See ante, at 1.

But if a competent person has a liberty interest to be free of unwanted medical treatment, as both the majority and JUSTICE o'CONNOR concede, it must be fundamental. "We are dealing here with [a decision] which involves one of the basic civil rights of man." Skinner v. Oklahoma ex rel. Williamson, 316 U.S. 535, 541 (1942) (invalidating a statute authorizing sterilization of certain felons). Whatever other liberties protected by the Due Process Clause are fundamental, "those liberties that are 'deeply rooted in this Nation's history and tradition'" are among them. Bowers v. Hardwick, 478 U.S. 186, 192 (1986) (quoting Moore v. East Cleveland, supra, at 503 (plurality opinion). "Such a tradition commands respect in part because the Constitution carries the gloss of history." Richmond Newspapers, Inc. v. Virginia, 448 U.S. 555, 589 (1980) (BRENNAN, J., concurring in judgment).

The right to be free from medical attention without consent, to determine what shall be done with one's own body, is deeply rooted in this Nation's traditions, as the majority acknowledges. See ante, at 5. This right has long been "firmly entrenched in American tort law" and is securely grounded in the earliest common law. Ibid. See also Mills v. Rogers, 457 U.S. 192, 294, n. 4 (1982) ("the right to refuse any medical treatment emerged from the doctrines of trespass and battery, which were applied to unauthorized touchings by a physician"). "'Anglo-American law starts with the premise of thorough-going self determination. It follows that each man is considered to be master of his own body, and he may, if he be of sound mind, expressly prohibit the performance of lifesaving surgery, or other medical treatment.'" Natanson v. Kline, 186 Kan. 393, 406-407, 350 P. 2d 1093, 1104 (1960). "The inviolability of the person" has been held as "sacred" and "carefully guarded" as any common law right. Union Pacific R. Co. v. Botsford, 141 U.S. 250, 251-252 (1891). thus, freedom from unwanted medical attention is unquestionably among those principles "so rooted in the traditions and conscience of our people as to be ranked as fundamental." Snyder v. Massachusetts, 291 U.S. 97, 105 (1934). [5]

That there may be serious consequences involved in refusal of the medical treatment at issue here does not vitiate the right under our common law tradition of medical self-determination. It is "a well-established rule of general law ... that it is the patient, not the physician, who ultimately decides if treatment - any treatment - is to be given at all. ... The rule has never been qualified in its application by either the nature or purposes of the treatment, or the gravity of the consequences of acceding to or foregoing it." Tune v. Walter Reed Army Medical Hospital, 602 F. Supp. 1452, 1455 (DC 1985). See also Downer v. Veilleux, 322 A. 2d 82, 91 (Me. 1974) ("The rationale of this rule lies in the fact that every competent adult has the right to forego treatment, or even cure, it it entails what for him are intolerable consequences or risks, however unwise his sense of values may be to others").[6]

No material distinction can be drawn between the treatment to which Nancy Cruzan continues to be subject - artificial nutrition and hydration - and any other medical treatment. See ante, at 2. (O'CONNOR, J., concurring). The artificial delivery of nutrition and hydration is undoubtedly medical treatment. The technique to which Nancy Cruzan is subject - artificial feeding through a gastrostomy tube - involves a tube implanted surgically into her stomach through incisions in her abdominal wall. It may obstruct the intestinal tract, erode and pierce the stomach wall or cause leakage of the stomach's contents into the abdominal cavity. See Page, Andrassy, & Sandler, Techniques in Delivery of Liquid Diets, in Nutrition in Clinical Surgery 66-67 (M. Deitel 2d ed. 1985). The tube can cause pneumonia from reflux of the stomach's contents into the lung. See Bernard & Forlaw, Complications and Their Prevention, in Enteral and Tube Feeding 553 (J. Rombeau & M. Caldwell eds. 1984). Typically, and in this case (see Tr. 377), commercially prepared formulas are used, rather than fresh food. See Matarese, Enteral Alimentation, in Surgical Nutrition 726 (J. Fischer ed. 1983). The type of formula and method of administration must be experimented with to avoid gastrointestinal problems. Id., at 748. The patient must be monitored daily by medical personnel as to weight, fluid intake and fluid output; blood tests must be done weekly. Id., at 749, 751.

Artificial delivery of food and water is regarded as medical treatment by the medical profession and the Federal Government.[7] According to the American Academy of Neurology, "[t]he artificial provision of nutrition and hydration is a form of medical treatment ... analogous to other forms of life-sustaining treatment, such as the use of the respirator. When a patient is unconscious, both a respirator and an artificial feeding device serve to support or replace normal bodily functions that are compromised as a result of the patient's illness." Position of the American Academy of Neurology on Certain Aspects of the care and Management of the Persistent Vegetative State Patient, 39 Neurology 125 (Ja. 1989). See also Council on Ethical and Judicial Affairs of the American Medical Association, Current Opinions, Opinion 2.20 (1989) ("Life-prolonging medical treatment includes medication and artifically or technologically supplied respiration, nutrition or hydration"); President's Commission 88 (life-sustaining treatment includes respirators, kidney dialysis machines, special feeding procedures). The Federal Government permits the cost of the medical devices and formulas used in enteral feeding to be reimbursed under Medicare. See Pub. L. 99-509, Section 9340, note following 42 U.S.C. Section 1395u, p. 592 (1982 ed., Supp. V). The formulas are regulated by the Federal Drug Administration as "medical foods," see 21 U.S.C. Section 360ee, and the feeding tubes are regulated as medical devices, 21 CFR Section 876.5980 (1989).

Nor does the fact that Nancy Cruzan is now incompetent deprive her of her fundamental rights See Youngberg v. Romeo, 457 U.S. 307, 315-316, 319 (1982) (holding that severely retarded man's liberty interests in safety, freedom from bodily restraint and reasonable training survive involuntary commitment); Parham v. J.R., 442 U.S. 584, 600 (1979) (recognizing a child's substantial liberty interest in not being confined unnecessarily for medical treatment); Jackson v. Indiana, 406 U.S. 715, 730 738 (1972) (holding that Indiana could not violate the due process and equal protection rights of a mentally retarded deaf mute by committing him for an indefinite amount of time simply because he was incompetent to stand trial on the criminal charges filed against him). As the majority recognizes, ante, at 16, the question is not whether an incompetent has constitutional rights, but how such rights may be exercised. As we explained in Thompson v. Oklahoma, 487 U.S. 815 (1988), "[t]he law must often adjust the manner in which it affords rights to those whose status renders them unable to exercise choice freely and rationally. Children, the insane, and those who are irreversibly ill with loss of brain function, for instance, all retain 'rights,' to be sure, but often such rights are only meaningful as they are exercised by agents acting with the best interests of their principals in mind." Id. at 825, n. 23 (emphasis added). "To deny [its] exercise because the patient is unconscious or incompetent would be to deny the right." Foody v. Manchester Memorial Hospital, 40 Conn. Super. 127, 133, 482 A. 2d 713, 718 (1984).

II

A

The right to be free from unwanted medical attention is a right to evaluate the potential benefit of treatment and its possible consequences according to one's own values and to make a personal decision whether to subject oneself to the intrusion. For a patient like Nancy Cruzan, the sole benefit of medical treatment is being kept metabolically alive. Neither artificial nutrition nor another form of medical treatment available today can cure or in any way ameliorate her condition.[8] Irreversibly vegetative patients are devoid of thought, emotion and sensation; they are permanently and completely unconscious. See n. 2, Supra.[9] As the President's Commission concluded in approving the withdrawal of life support equipment from irreversibly vegetative patients:

> "[T]reatment ordinarily aims to benefit a patient through preserving life, relieving pain and suffering, protecting against disability, and returning maximally effective functioning. If a prognosis of permanent unconsciousness is correct, however, continued treatment cannot confer such benefits. Pain and suffering are absent, as are joy, satisfaction, and pleasure. Disability is total and no return to an even minimal level of social or human functioning is possible." President's Commission 181-182.

41

There are also affirmative reasons why someone like Nancy might choose to forgo artificial nutrition and hydration under these circumstances. Dying is personal. And it is profound. For many, the thought of an ignoble end, steeped in decay, is abhorrent. A quiet, proud death, bodily integrity intact, is a matter of extreme consequence. "In certain, thankfully rare, circumstances the burden of maintaining the corporeal existence degrades the very humanity it was meant to serve." Brophy v. New England Sinai Hospital, Inc., 398 Mass. 417, 434, 497 N.E. 2d 626, 635-636 (1986) (finding the subject of the proceeding "in a condition which [he] has indicated he would consider to be degrading and without human dignity" and holding that "[t]he duty of the State to preserve life must encompass a recognition of an individual's right to avoid circumstances in which the individual himself would feel that efforts to sustain life demean or degrade his humanity"). Another court, hearing a similar case, noted:

> "It is apparent from the testimony that what was on [the patient's] mind was not only the invasiveness of life-sustaining systems, such as the [nasogastric] tube, upon the integrity of his body. It was also the utter helplessness of the permanently comatose person, the wasting of a once strong body, and the submission of the most private bodily functions to the attention of others." In re Gardner, 534 A. 2d 947, 953 (Me. 1987).

Such conditions are, for many, humiliating to contemplate, [10] as is visiting a prolonged and anguished vigil on one's parents, spouse, and children. A long, drawn-out death can have a debilitating effect on family members. See Carnwath & Johnson, Psychiatric Morbidity Among Spouses of Patients With Stroke, 294 Brit. Med. J. 409 (1987); Livingston, Families Who Care, 291 Brit. Med. J. 919 (1985). For some, the idea of being remembered in their persistent vegetative states rather than as they were before their illness or accident may be very disturbing.[11]

B

Although the right to be free of unwanted medical intervention, like other constitutionally protected interests, may not be absolute, [12] no State interest could outweigh the rights of an individual in Nancy Cruzan's position. Whatever a State's possible interests in mandating life-support treatment under other circumstances, there is no good to be obtained here by Missouri's insistence that Nancy Cruzan remain on life-support systems if it is indeed her wish not to do so. Missouri does not claim, nor could it, that society as a whole will be benefited by Nancy's receiving medical treatment. No third party's situation will be improved and no harm to others will be averted. Cf. nn. 6 and 8, supra.[13]

The only state interest asserted here is a general interest in the preservation of life.[14] But the State has no legitimate general interest in someone's life, completely abstracted from the interest of the person living that life, that could outweigh the person's choice to avoid medical treatment. "[T]he regulation of constitutionally protected decisions ... must be predicated on legitimate state concerns other than disagreement with the choice the individual has made ... . Otherwise, the interest in liberty protected by the Due Process Clause would be nullity." Hodgson v. Minnesota, ____ U.S. ____, ____ (1990) (Opinion of STEVENS, J.) (slip op., at 14) (emphasis added). Thus, the State's general interest in life must accede to Nancy Cruzan's particularized and intense interest in self-determination in her choice of medical treatment. There is simply nothing legitimately within the State's purview to be gained by superseding her decision.

Moreover, there may be considerable danger that Missouri's rule of decision would impair rather than serve any interest the State does have in sustaining life. Current medical practice recommends use of heroic measures if there is a scintilla of a chance that the patient will recover, on the assumption that the measures will be discontinued should the patient improve. When the President's Commission in 1982 approved the withdrawal of life support equipment from irreversibly vegetative patients, it explained that "[a]n even more troubling wrong occurs when a treatment that might save life or improve health is not started because the health care personnel are afraid that they will find it very difficult to stop the treatment if, as is fairly like, it proves to be of little benefit and greatly burdens the patient." President's Commission 75. A New Jersey court recognized that families as well as doctors might be discouraged by an inability to stop life-support measures from "even attempting certain types of care [which] could thereby force them into hasty and premature decisions to allow a patient to die." In re Conroy, 98 N.J. 321, 370, 486 A. 2d 1209, 1234, (1985). See also Brief for American Academy of Neurology as Amicus Cruae 9 (expressing same concern).[15]

III

This is not to say that the State has no legitimate interests to assert here. As the majority recognizes, ante, at 17, Missouri has a parens patriae interest in providing Nancy Cruzan, now incompetent, with as accurate as possible a determination of how she would exercise her rights under these circumstances. Second, if and when it is determined that Nancy Cruzan would want to continue treatment, the State may legitimately assert an interest in providing that treatment. But until Nancy's wishes have been determined, the only state interest that may be asserted is an interest in safeguarding the accuracy of that determination.

Accuracy, therefore, must be our touchstone. Missouri may constitutionally impose only those procedural requirements that serve to enhance the accuracy of a determination of Nancy Cruzan's wishes or are at least consistent with an accurate determination. The Missouri "safeguard" that the court upholds today does not meet that standard. The determination needed in this context is whether the incompetent person would choose to live in a persistent vegetative state on life-support or to avoid this medical treatment. Missouri's rule of decision imposes a markedly asymmetrical evidentiary burden. Only evidence of specific statements of treatment choice made by the patient when competent is admissible to support a finding that the patient, now in a persistent vegetative state, would wish to avoid further medical treatment. Moreover, this evidence must be clear and convincing. No

43

proof is required to support a finding that the incompetent person would wish to continue treatment.

A

The majority offers several justifications for Missouri's heightened evidentiary standard. First, the majority explains that the State may constitutionally adopt this rule to govern determinations of an incompetent's wishes in order to advance the State's substantive interests, including its unqualified interest in the preservation of human life. See ante, at 17-18, and n. 10. Missouri's evidentiary standard, however, cannot rest on the State's own interest in a particular substantive result. To be sure, courts have long erected clear and convincing evidence standards to place the greater risk of erroneous decisions on those bringing disfavored claims.[16] In such cases, however, the choice to discourage certain claims was a legitimate, constitutional policy choice. In contrast, Missouri has no such power to disfavor a choice by Nancy Cruzan to avoid medical treatment, because Missouri has no legitimate interest in providing Nancy with treatment until it is established that this represents her choice. See supra, at 13-14. Just as a State may not override Nancy's choice directly, it may not do so indirectly through the imposition of a procedural rule.

Second, the majority offers two explanations for why Missouri's clear and convincing evidence standard is a means of enhancing accuracy, but neither is persuasive. The majority initially argues that a clear and convincing evidence standard is necessary to compensate for the possibility that such proceedings will lack the "guarantee of accurate factfinding that the adversary process brings with it," citing Ohio v. Akron Center for Reproductive Health, ____ U.S. ____, ____ (1990) (upholding a clear and convincing evidence standard for an ex parte proceeding). Ante, at 17. Without supporting the Court's decision in that case, I note that the proceeding to determine an incompetent's wishes is quite different from a proceeding to determine whether a minor may bypass notifying her parents before undergoing an abortion on the ground that she is mature enough to make the decision or that the abortion is in her best interests.

An adversarial proceeding is of particular importance when one side has a strong personal interest which needs to be counterbalanced to assure the court that the questions will be fully explored. A minor who has a strong interest in obtaining permission for an abortion without notifying her parents may come forward whether or not society would be satisfied that she has made the decision with the seasoned judgment of an adult. The proceeding here is of a different nature. Barring venal motives, which a trial court has the means of ferreting out, the decision to come forward to request a judicial order to stop treatment represents a slowly and carefully considered resolution by at least one adult and more frequently several adults that discontinuation of treatment is the patient's wish.

In addition, the bypass procedure at issue in Akron, supra, is ex parte and secret. The court may not notify the minor's parents, siblings or friends. No one may be present to submit evidence unless brought forward by the minor herself. In contract, the proceeding to determine Nancy Cruzan's wishes was neither _ex parte_ nor secret. In a hearing to determine the treatment preferences of an incompetent person, a court is not limited to adjusting burdens of proof as its only means of protecting against a possible imbalance. Indeed, any concern that those who come forward will present a one-sided view would be better addressed by appointing a guardian ad litem, who could use the State's powers of discovery to gather and present evidence regarding the patient's wishes. A guardian ad litem's task is to uncover any conflicts of interest and ensure that each party likely to have relevant evidence is consulted and brought forward - for example, other members of the family, friends, clergy, and doctors. _See, e.g.,_ _In re Colyer_, 99 Wash. 2d 114, 133, 660 P. 2d 738, 748-749 (1983). Missouri's heightened evidentiary standard attempts to achieve balance by discounting evidence; the guardian ad litem technique achieves balance by probing for additional evidence. Where, as here, the family members, friends, doctors and guardian ad litem agree, it is not because the process has failed, as the majority suggests. _See ante_, at 17, n. 9. It is because there is no genuine dispute as to Nancy's preference.

The majority next argues that where, as here, important individual rights are at stake, a clear and convincing evidence standard has long been held to be an appropriate means of enhancing accuracy, citing decisions concerning what process an individual is due before he can be deprived of a liberty interest. _See ante_, at 18-19. In those cases, however, this Court imposed a clear and convincing standard as a constitutional minimum on the basis of its evaluation that one side's interests clearly outweighed the second side's interests and therefore the second side should bear the risk of error. _See Santosky v._ _Kramer_, 455 U.S. 745, 753, 766-767 (1982) (requiring a clear and convincing evidence standard for termination of parental rights because the parent's interest is fundamental but the State has no legitimate interest in termination unless the parent is unfit, and finding that the State's interest in finding the best home for the child does not arise until the parent has been found unfit); _Addington v. Texas_, 441 U.S. 418, 426-427 (1979) (requiring clear and convincing evidence in an involuntary commitment hearing because the interest of the individual far outweighs that of a State, which has no legitimate interest in confining individuals who are not mentally ill and do not pose a danger to themselves or others). Moreover, we have always recognized that shifting the risk of error reduces the likelihood of errors in one direction at the cost of increasing the likelihood of errors in the other. _See Addington_, _supra_, at 423 (contrasting heightened standards of proof to a preponderance standard in which the two sides "share the risk of error in roughly equal fashion" because society does not favor one outcome over the other); In the cases cited by the majority, the imbalance imposed by a heightened evidentiary standard was not only acceptable but required because the standard was deployed to protect an individual's exercise of a fundamental right, as the majority admits, _ante_, at 18, n. 10. In contrast, the Missouri court imposed a clear and convincing standard as an obstacle to the exercise of a fundamental right.

The majority claims that the allocation of the risk of error is justified because it is more important not to terminate life-support for someone who would wish it continued than to honor the wishes of someone who would not. An erroneous decision to terminate life-support is irrevocable, says the majority, while an erroneous decision not to terminate "results in a maintenance of the status quo." See ante, at 19.[17] But, from the point of view of the patient, an erroneous decision in either direction is irrevocable. An erroneous decision to terminate artificial nutrition and hydration, to be sure, will lead to failure of that last remnant of physiological life, the brain stem, and result in complete brain death. An erroneous decision not to terminate life-support, however, robs a patient of the very qualities protected by the right to avoid unwanted medical treatment. His own degraded existence is perpetuated; his family's suffering is protracted; the memory he leaves behind becomes more and more distorted.

Even a later decision to grant him his wish cannot undo the intervening harm. But a later decision is unlikely in any event. "[T]he discovery of new evidence," to which the majority refers, ibid., is more hypothetical than plausible. The majority also misconceives the relevance of the possibility of "advancements in medical science," ibid., by treating it as a reason to force someone to continue medical treatment against his will. The possibility of a medical miracle is indeed part of the calculus, but it is a part of the patient's calculus. If current research suggests that some hope for cure or even moderate improvement is possible within the life-span projected, this is a factor that should be and would be accorded significant weight in assessing what the patient himself would choose.[18]

B

Even more than its heightened evidentiary standard, the Missouri court's categorical exclusion of relevant evidence dispenses with any semblence of accurate factfinding. The court adverted to no evidence supporting its decision, but held that no clear and convincing, inherently reliable evidence had been presented to show that Nancy would want to avoid further treatment. In doing so, the court failed to consider statements Nancy had made to family members and a close friend.[19] The court also failed to consider testimony from Nancy's mother and sister that they were certain that Nancy would want to discontinue to artificial nutrition and hydration,[20] even after the court found that Nancy's family was loving and without malignant motive. See 760 S.W. 2d, at 412. The court also failed to consider the conclusions of the guardian ad litem, appointed by the trial court, that there was clear and convincing evidence that Nancy would want to discontinue medical treatment and that this was in her best interests. id., at 444 (Higgins, J., dissenting from denial of rehearing); Brief for Respondent Guardian Ad Litem 2-3. The court did not specifically define what kind of evidence it would consider clear and convincing, but its general discussion suggests that only a living will or equivalently formal directive from the patient when competent would meet this standard. See 760 S.W. 2d, at 424-425.

Too few people execute living wills or equivalently formal directives for such an evidentiary rule to ensure adequately that the wishes of incompetent persons will be honored.[21] While it might be a wise social policy to encourage people to furnish such instructions, no general conclusion about a patient's choice can be drawn from the absence of formalities. The probability of becoming irreversibly vegetative is so low that many people may not feel an urgency to marshal formal evidence of their preferences. Some may not wish to dwell on their own physical deterioration and mortality. Even someone with a resolute determination to avoid life-support under circumstances such as Nancy's would still need to know that such things as living wills exist and how to execute one. Often legal help would be necessary, especially given the majority's apparent willingness to permit States to insist that a person's wishes are not truly known unless the particular medical treatment is specified. See ante, at 21.

As a California appellate court observed: "The lack of generalized public awareness of the statutory scheme and the typically human characteristics of procrastination and reluctance to contemplate the need for such arrangements however makes this a tool which will all too often go unused by those who might desire it." Barber v. Superior Court, 147 Cal. App. 3d 1006, 1015, 194 Cal. Rptr. 484, 489 (1983). When a person tells family or close friends that she does not want her life sustained artificially, she is "express[ing] her wishes in the only terms familiar to her, and ... as clearly as a lay person should be asked to express them. To require more is unrealistic, and for all practical purposes, it precludes the rights of patients to forego life-sustaining treatment." In re O'Connor, 72 N.Y. 2d 517, 551, 531 N.E. 2d 607, 626 (1988) (Simons, J., dissenting).[22] When Missouri enacted a living will statute, it specifically provided that the absence of a living will does not warrant a presumption that a patient wishes continued medical treatment. See n. 15, supra. Thus, apparently not even Missouri's own legislature believes that a person who does not execute a living will fails to do so because he wishes continuous medical treatment under all circumstances.

The testimony of close friends and family members, on the other hand, may often be the best evidence available of what the patient's choice would be. It is they with whom the patient most likely will have discussed such questions and they who know the patient best. "Family members have a unique knowledge of the patient which is vital to any decision on his or her behalf." Newman, Treatment Refusals for the Critically and Terminally Ill: Proposed Rules for the Family, the Physician, and the State, 3 N.Y.L.S. Human Rights Annual 35, 46 (1985). The Missouri court's decision to ignore this whole category of testimony is also at odds with the practices of other States. See, e.g., In re Peter, 108 N.J. 365, 529 A. 2d 419 (1987), Brophy v. New England Sinai Hospital, Inc., 398 Mass. 417, 497 N.E. 2d 626 (1986); In re Severns, 425 A. 2d 156 (Del. Ch. 1980).

The Missouri court's disdain for Nancy's statements in serious conversations not long before her accident, for the opinion of Nancy's family and friends as to her values, beliefs and certain choice, and even for the opinion of an outside objective factfinder appointed by the State evinces a disdain for Nancy Cruzan's own right to choose. The rules by which an incompetent person's wishes are determined must

47

represent every effort to determine those wishes. The rule that the Missouri court adopted and that this Court upholds, however, skews the result away from a determination that as accurately as possible reflects the individual's own preferences and beliefs. It is a rule that transforms human beings into passive subjects of medical technology.

> "[M]edical care decisions must be guided by the individual patient's interests and values. Allowing persons to determine their own medical treatment is an important way in which society respects persons as individuals. Moreover, the respect due to persons as individuals does not diminish simply because they have become incapable of participating in treatment decisions. ... [I]t is still possible for others to make a decision that reflects [the patient's] interests more closely than would a purely technological decision to do whatever is possible. Lacking the ability to decide, [a patient] has a right to a decision that takes his interests into account." In re Drabick, 200 Cal. App. 3d 185, 208; 245 Cal. Rptr. 840, 854-855 (1988).

C

I do not suggest that States must sit by helplessly if the choices of incompetent patients are in danger of being ignored. See ante, at 17. Even if the Court had ruled that Missouri's rule of decision is unconstitutional, as I believe it should have, States would nevertheless remain free to fashion procedural protections to safeguard the interests of incompetents under these circumstances. The Constitution provides merely a framework here: protections must be genuinely aimed at ensuring decisions commensurate with the will of the patient, and must be reliable as instruments to that end. Of the many States which have instituted such protections, Missouri is virtually the only one to have fashioned a rule that lessens the likelihood of accurate determinations. In contrast, nothing in the Constitution prevents States from reviewing the advisability of a family decision, by requiring a court proceeding or by appointing an impartial guardian ad litem.

There are various approaches to determining an incompetent patient's treatment choice in use by the several States today and there may be advantages and disadvantages to each and other approaches not yet envisioned. The choice, in largest part, is and should be left to the States, so long as each State is seeking, in a reliable manner, to discover what the patient would want. But with such momentous interests in the balance, States must avoid procedures that will prejudice the decision. "To err either way - to keep a person alive under circumstances under which he would rather have been allowed to die, or to allow that person to die when he would have chosen to cling to life - would be deeply unfortunate." In re Conroy, 98 N.J., at 343, 486 A. 2d, at 1220.

D

Finally, I cannot agree with the majority that where it is not possible to determine what choice an incompetent patient would make, a State's roles as _parens patriae_ permits the State automatically to make that choice itself. _See ante,_ at 22 (explaining that the Due Process Clause does not require a State to confide the decision to "anyone but the patient herself"). Under fair rules of evidence, it is improbable that a court could not determine what the patient's choice would be. Under the rule of decision adopted by Missouri and upheld today by this Court, such occasions might be numerous. But in neither case does it follow that it is constitutionally acceptable for the State invariably to assume the role of deciding for the patient. A State's legitimate interest in safeguarding a patient's choice cannot be furthered by simply appropriating it.

The majority justifies its position by arguing that, while close family members may have a strong feeling about the question, "there is no automatic assurance that the view of close family members will necessarily be the same as the patient's would have been had she been confronted with the prospect of her situation while competent." _Ibid_. I cannot quarrel with this observation. But it leads only to another question: Is there any reason to suppose that a State is _more_ likely to make the choice that the patient would have made than someone who knew the patient intimately? To ask this is to answer it. As the New Jersey Supreme Court observed: "Family members are best qualified to make substituted judgments for incompetent patients not only because of their peculiar grasp of the patient's approach to life, but also because of their special bonds with him or her. ... It is ... they who treat the patient as a person, rather than a symbol of a cause." _In re Jobes,_ 108 N.J. 394, 416, 529 A. 2d 434, 445 (1987). The State, in contrast, is a stranger to the patient.

A State's inability to discern an incompetent patient's choice still need not mean that a State is rendered powerless to protect that choice. But I would find that the Due Process Clause prohibits a State from doing more than that. A State may ensure that the person who makes the decision on the patient's behalf is the one whom the patient himself would most likely have chosen as proxy or leave the decision to the patient's family.[23]

IV

As many as 10,000 patients are being maintained in persistent vegetative states in the United States, and the number is expected to increase significantly in the near future. _See_ Cranford, _supra_ n. 2, at 27, 31. Medical technology, developed over the past 20 or so years, is often capable of resuscitating people after they have stopped breathing or their hearts have stopped beating. Some of those people are brought fully back to life. Two decades ago, those who were not and could not swallow and digest food, died. Intravenous solutions could not provide sufficient calories to maintain people for more than a short time. Today, various forms of artificial feeding have been developed that are able to keep people metabolically alive for years, even decades. _See_ Spencer & Palmisano, Specialized Nutritional Support of Patients - A Hospital's Legal Duty?, 11 Quality Rev. Bull. 160, 160-161 (1985). In addition, in this century, chronic or degenerative ailments have replaced communicable diseases as the primary causes of death. See R. Weir, Abating Treatment with Critically Ill Patients 12-13 (1989); President's Commission 15-16. The 80% of Americans who die in hospitals are "likely to meet their end ... `in a sedated or comatose state; betubed nasally, abdominally and intravenously; and far more like manipulated objects than like moral subjects.'"[24] A fifth of all adults surviving to age 80 will suffer a progressive dementing disorder prior to death. See Cohen & Eisdorfer, Dementing Disorders, in The Practice of Geriatrics 194 (E. Calkins, P. Davis, & A, Ford eds. 1986).

"[L]aw, equity and justice must not themselves quail and be helpless in the face of modern technological marvels presenting questions hitherto unthought of." In re Quinlan, 70 N.J. 10, 44, 355 A. 2d 647, 665, cert. denied, 429 U.S. 922 (1976). The new medical technology can reclaim those who would have been irretrievably lost a few decades ago and restore them to active lives. For Nancy Cruzan, it failed, and for others with wasting incurable disease it may be doomed to failure. In these unfortunate situations, the bodies and preferences and memories of the victims do not escheat to the State; nor does our Constitution permit the State or any other government to commandeer them. No singularity of feeling exists upon which such a government might confidently rely as parens patriae. The President's Commission, after years of research, concluded:

> "In few areas of health care are people's evaluations of their experiences so varied and uniquely personal as in their assessments of the nature and value of the processes associated with dying. For some, every moment of life is of inestimable value; for others, life without some desired level of mental or physical ability is worthless or burdensome. A moderate degree of suffering may be an important means of personal growth and religious experience to one person, but only frightening or despicable to another." President's Commission 276.

Yet Missouri and this Court have displaced Nancy's own assessment of the processes associated with dying. They have discarded evidence of her will, ignored her values, and deprived her of the right to a decision as closely approximating her own choice as humanly possible. They have done so disingenuously in her name, and openly in Missouri's own. That Missouri and this Court may truly be motivated only by concern for incompetent patients makes no matter. As one of our most prominent jurists warned us decades ago: "Experience should teach us to be most on our guard to protect liberty when the government's purposes are beneficent. ... The greatest dangers to liberty lurk in insidious encroachment by men of zeal, well meaning but without understanding." Olmstead v. United States, 277 U.S. 438, 479 (1928) (Brandeis, J., dissenting).

I respectfully dissent.

JUSTICE STEVENS, dissenting.

Our Constitution is born of the proposition that all legitimate governments must secure the equal right of every person to "Life, Liberty, and the pursuit of Happiness."[1] In the ordinary case we quite naturally assume that these three ends are compatible, mutually enhancing, and perhaps even coincident.

The Court would make an exception here. It permits the State's abstract, undifferentiated interest in the preservation of life to overwhelm the best interests of Nancy Beth Cruzan, interests which would, according to an undisputed finding, be served by allowing her guardians to exercise her constitutional right to discontinue medical treatment. Ironically, the Court reaches this conclusion despite endorsing three significant propositions which should save it from any such dilemma. First, a competent individual's decision to refuse life-sustaining medical procedures is an aspect of liberty protected by the Due Process Clause of the Fourteenth Amendment. See ante, at 14-15. Second, upon a proper evidentiary showing, a qualified guardian may make that decision on behalf of an incompetent ward. See, e.g., ante, at 20. Third, in answering the important question presented by this tragic case, it is wise "not to attempt by any general statement, to cover every possible phase of the subject." See ante, at 13 (citation omitted). Together, these considerations suggest that Nancy Cruzan's liberty to be free from medical treatment must be understood in light of the facts and circumstances particular to her.

I would so hold: in my view, the Constitution requires the State to care for Nancy Cruzan's life in a way that gives appropriate respect to her own best interests.

I

This case is the first in which we consider whether, and how, the Constitution protects the liberty of seriously ill patients to be free from life-sustaining medical treatment. So put, the question is both general and profound. We need not, however, resolve the question in the abstract. Our responsibility as judges both enables and compels us to treat the problem as it is illuminated by the facts of the controversy before us.

The most important of those facts are these: "clear and convincing evidence" established that Nancy Cruzan is "oblivious to her environment except for reflexive responses to sound and perhaps to painful stimuli", that "she has no cognitive or reflexive ability to swallow food or water" that "she will never recover" these abilities; and that her "cerebral cortical atrophy is irreversible, permanent, progressive and ongoing." App. to Pet. for Cert. A94-A95. Recovery and consciousness are impossible; the highest cognitive brain function that can be hoped for is a grimace in "recognition of ordinarily painful stimuli" or an "apparent response to sound." Id., at A95.[2]

After thus evaluating Nancy Cruzan's medical condition, the trial judge next examined how the interests of third parties would be affected if Nancy's parents were allowed to withdraw the gastrostomy tube that had been implanted in their daughter. His findings make it clear that the parents' request had no economic motivation,[3] and that granting their request would neither adversely affect any innocent third parties nor breach the ethical standards of the medical profession.[4] He then considered, and rejected, a religious objection to his decision,[5] and explained why he concluded that the ward's constitutional "right to liberty" outweighed the general public policy on which the State relied:

> "There is a fundamental natural right expressed in our Constitution as the 'right to liberty,' which permits an individual to refuse or direct the withholding or withdrawal of artificial death prolonging procedures when the person has no more cognitive brain function than our Ward and all the physicians agree there is no hope of further recovery while the deterioration of the brain continues with further overall worsening physical contractures. To the extent that the statute or public policy prohibits withholding or withdrawal of nutrition and hydration or euthanasia or mercy killing, if such be the definition, under all circumstances, arbitrarily and with no exceptions, it is in violation of our ward's constitutional rights by depriving her of liberty without due process of law. To decide otherwise that medical treatment once undertaken must be continued irrespective of its lack of success or benefit to the patient in effect gives one's body to medical science without their consent.

"The Co-guardians are required only to exercise their legal authority to act in the best interests of their Ward as they discharge their duty and are free to act or not with this authority as they may determine." Id., at A98-A99 (footnotes omitted).

II

Because he believed he had a duty to do so, the independent guardian ad litem appealed the trial court's order to the Missouri Supreme Court. In that appeal, however, the guardian advised the court that he did not disagree with the trial court's decision. Specifically, he endorsed the critical finding that "it was in Nancy Cruzan's best interests to have the tube feeding discontinued."[6]

That important conclusion thus was not disputed by the litigants. One might reasonably suppose that it would be dispositive: if Nancy Cruzan has no interest in continued treatment, and if she has a liberty interest in being free from unwanted treatment, and if the cessation of treatment would have no adverse impact on third parties, and if no reason exists to doubt the good faith of Nancy's parents, then what possible basis could the State have for insisting upon continued medical treatment? Yet, instead of questioning or endorsing the trial court's conclusions about Nancy Cruzan's interests, the State Supreme Court largely ignored them.

The opinion of that court referred to four different state interests that have been identified in other somewhat similar cases,

52

but acknowledged that only the State's general interest in "the preservation of life" was implicated by this case.[7] It defined that interest as follows:

> "The state's interest in life embraces two separate concerns: an interest in the prolongation of the life of the individual patient and an interest in the sanctity of life itself." Cruzan v. Harmon, 760 S.W. 2d 408, 419 (1988).

Although the court did not characterize this interest as absolute, it repeatedly indicated that it outweighs any countervailing interest that is based on the "quality of life" of any individual patient.[8] In the view of the state-court majority, that general interest is strong enough to foreclose any decision to refuse treatment for an incompetent person unless that person had previously evidenced, in a clear and convincing terms, such a decision for herself. The best interests of the incompetent individual who had never confronted the issue - or perhaps had been incompetent since birth - are entirely irrelevant and unprotected under the reasoning of the State Supreme Court's four-judge majority.

The three dissenting judges found Nancy Cruzan's interests compelling. They agreed with the trial court's evaluation of state policy. In his persuasive dissent, Judge Blackmar explained that decisions about the care of chronically ill patients were traditionally private:

> "My disagreement with the principal opinion lies fundamentally in its emphasis on the interest of and the role of the state, represented by the Attorney General. Decisions about prolongation of life are of recent origin. For most of the world's history, and presently in most parts of the world, such decision would never arise because the technology would not be available. Decisions about medical treatment have customarily been made by the patient, or by those closest to the patient if the patient, because of youth or infirmity, is unable to make the decisions. This is nothing new in substituted decisionmaking. The state is seldom called upon to be the decisionmaker.

> "I would not accept the assumption, inherent in the principal opinion, that, with our advanced technology, the state must necessarily become involved in a decision about using extraordinary measures to prolong life. Decisions of this kind are made daily by the patient or relatives, on the basis of medical advise and their conclusion as to what is best. Very few cases reach court, and I doubt whether this case would be before us but for the fact that Nancy lies in a state hospital. I do not place primary emphasis on the patient's expressions, except possibly in the very unusual case, of which I find no example in the books, in which the patient expresses a view that all available life supports should be made use of. Those closest to the patient are best positioned to make judgments about the patient's best interest." Id., at 428.

Judge Blackmar then argued that Missouri's policy imposed upon dying individuals and their families a controversial and objectionable view of life's meaning:

"It is unrealistic to say that the preservation of life is an absolute, without regard to the quality of life. I make this statement only in the context of a case in which the trial judge has found that there is no chance for amelioration of Nancy's condition. The principal opinion accepts this conclusion. It is appropriate to consider the quality of life in making decisions about the extraordinary medical treatment. Those who have made decisions about such matters without resort to the courts certainly consider the quality of life, and balance this against the unpleasant consequences to the patient. There is evidence that Nancy may react to pain stimuli. If she has any awareness of her surroundings, her life must be a living hell. She is unable to express herself or to do anything at all to alter her situation. Her parents, who are her closest relatives, are best able to feel for her and to decide what is best for her. The state should not substitute its decisions for theirs. Nor am I impressed with the crypto-philosophers cited in the principal opinion, who declaim about the sanctity of any life without regard to its quality. They dwell in ivory towers." id., at 429.

Finally, Judge Blackmar concluded that the Missouri policy was illegitimate because it treats life as a theoretical abstraction, severed from, and indeed opposed to, the person of Nancy Cruzan.

"The Cruzan family appropriately came before the court seeking relief. The circuit judge properly found the facts and applied the law. His factual findings are supported by the record and his legal conclusions by overwhelming weight of authority. The principal opinion attempts to establish absolutes, but does so at the expense of human factors. In so doing it unnecessarily subjects Nancy and those close to her to continuous torture which no family should be forced to endure." Id., at 429-430.

Although Judge Blackmar did not frame his argument as such, it propounds a sound constitutional objection to the Missouri majority's reasoning: Missouri's regulation is an unreasonable intrusion upon traditionally private matters encompassed within the liberty protected by the Due Process Clause.

The portion of this Court's opinion that considers the merits of this case is similarly unsatisfactory. It, too, fails to respect the best interests of the patient.[9] It, too, relies on what is tantamount to a waiver rationale: the dying patient's best interests are put to one side and the entire inquiry is focused on her prior expressions of intent.[10] An innocent person's constitutional right to be free from unwanted medical treatment is thereby categorically limited to those patients who had the foresight to make an unambiguous statement of their wishes while competent. The Court's decision affords no protection to children, to young people who are victims of unexpected accidents or illnesses, or to the countless thousands of elderly persons who either fail to decide, or fail to explain, how they want to be treated if they should experience a similar fate. Because Nancy Beth Cruzan did not have the foresight to preserve her constitutional right in a living will, or some comparable "clear an convincing" alternative, her right is gone forever and her fate is in the hands of the state legislature instead of in those of her family, her independent neutral guardian ad litem, and an impartial judge - all of whom agree on the course of action that is in her best interests. The Court's willingness to find a waiver of this constitutional right reveals a distressing misunderstanding of the importance of individual liberty.

III

It is perhaps predictable that courts might undervalue the liberty at stake here. Because death is so profoundly personal, public reflection upon it is unusual. As this sad case shows, however, such reflection must become more common if we are to deal responsibly with the modern circumstances of death. Medical advances have altered the physiological conditions of death in ways that may be alarming: highly invasive treatment may perpetuate human existence through a merger of body and machine that some might reasonably regard as an insult to life rather than as its continuation. But those same advances, and the reorganization of medical care accompanying the new science and technology, have also transformed the political and social conditions of death: people are less likely to die at home, and more likely to die in relatively public places, such as hospitals or nursing homes.[11]

Ultimate questions that might once have been dealt with in intimacy by a family and its physician[12] have now become the concern of institutions. When the institution is a state hospital, as it is in this case, the government itself becomes involved.[13] Dying nonetheless remains a part of "the life which characteristically has its place in the home," Poe v. Ullman, 367 U.S. 497, 551 (1961) (Harlan, J., dissenting). The "integrity of that life is something so fundamental that it has been found to draw to its protection the principles of more than one explicitly granted Constitutional right," id., at 551-552, and our decisions have demarcated a "private realm of family life which the state cannot enter." Prince v. Massachusetts, 321 U.S. 158, 166-167 (1944). The physical boundaries of the home, of course, remain crucial guarantors of the life within it. See e.g., Payton v. New York, 445 U.S. 573, 589 (1980); Stanley v. Georgia, 394 U.S. 557, 565 (1969). Nevertheless, this Court has long recognized that the liberty to make the decisions and choices constitutive of private life is so fundamental to our "concept of ordered liberty," Palko v. Connecticut, 302 U.S. 319, 325 (1937), that those choices must occasionally be afforded more direct protection. See e.g., Meyer v. Nebraska, 262 U.S. 390 (1923); Griswold v. Connecticut, 381 U.S. 479 (1965); Roe v. Wade, 410 U.S. 113 (1973); Thornburgh v. American College of Obstetricians and Gynecologists, 476 U.S. 747, 772-782 (1986) (STEVENS, J., concurring).

Respect for these choices has guided our recognition of rights pertaining to bodily integrity. The constitutional decisions identifying those rights, like the common-law tradition upon which they built,[14] are mindful that the "makers of our Constitution ... recognized the significance of man's spiritual nature." Olmstead v. United States, 277 U.S. 438, 478 (1928) (Brandeis, J., dissenting). It may truly be said that "our nations of liberty are inextricably entwined with our idea of physical freedom and self determination." Ante, at 1 (O'CONNOR, J., concurring). Thus we have construed the Due Process Clause to preclude physically invasive recoveries of evidence not only because such procedures are "brutal" but also because they are "offensive to human dignity." Rochin v. California, 342 U.S. 165, 174 (1952). We have interpreted the Constitution to interpose barriers to a State's efforts to sterilize some criminals not only because the proposed punishment would do "irreparable injury" to bodily integrity, but because "[m]arriage and procreation" concern "the basic civil rights of man." Skinner v. Oklahoma el rel. Williamson, 316 U.S. 535, 541 (1942). The sanctity, and individual privacy, of the human body is obviously fundamental to liberty. "Every violation of a person's bodily integrity is an invasion of his or her liberty." Washington v. Harper, 494 U.S. _____, ____ (1990) (STEVENS, J., concurring in part and dissenting in part). Yet, just as the constitutional protection for the "physical curtilage of the home ... is surely ... a result of solicitude to protect the privacies of the life within," Poe v. Ullman, 367 U.S., at 551 (Harlan, J., dissenting), so too the constitutional protection for the human body is surely inseparable from concern for the mind and spirit that dwell therein.

It is against this background of decisional law, and the constitutional tradition which it illuminates, that the right to be free from unwanted life-sustaining medical treatment must be understood. That right presupposes no abandonment of the desire for life. Nor is it reducible to a protection against batteries undertaken in the name of treatment, or to a guarantee against the infliction of bodily discomfort. Choices about death touch the core of liberty. Our duty, and the concomitant freedom, to come to terms with the conditions of our own mortality are undoubtedly "so rooted in the traditions and conscience of our people as to be ranked as fundamental," Snyder v. Massachusetts, 291 U.S. 97, 105 (1934), and indeed are essential incidents of the unalienable rights to life and liberty endowed us by our Creator. See Meachum v. Fano, 427 U.S. 215, 230 (1976) (STEVENS, J., dissenting).

The more precise constitutional significance of death is difficult to describe; not much may be said with confidence about death unless it is said from faith, and that alone is reason enough to protect the freedom to conform choices about death to individual conscience. We may also, however, justly assume that death is not life's simple opposite, or its necessary terminus,[15] but rather its completion. Our ethical tradition has long regarded an appreciation of mortality as essential to understanding life's significance. It may, in fact, be impossible to live for anything without being prepared to die for something. Certainly there was no disdain for life in Nathan Hale's most famous declaration or in Patrick Henry's; their words instead bespeak a passion for life that forever preserves their own lives in the memories of their countrymen.[16] From such "honored dead we take increased devotion to that cause for which they gave the last full measure of devotion."[17]

These considerations cast into stark relief the injustice, and unconstitutionality, of Missouri's treatment of Nancy Beth Cruzan. Nancy Cruzan's death, when it comes, cannot be an historic act of heroism; it will inevitably be the consequence of her tragic accident. But Nancy Cruzan's interest in life, no less than that of any other person, includes an interest in how she will be thought of after her death by those whose opinions mattered to her. There can be no doubt that her life made her dear to her family, and to others. How she dies will affect how that life is remembered. The trial court's order authorizing Nancy's parents to cease their daughter's treatment would have permitted the family that cares for Nancy to bring to a close her tragedy and her death. Missouri's objection to that order subordinates Nancy's body, her family, and the lasting significance of her life to the State's own interests. The decision we review thereby interferes with constitutional interests of the highest order.

To be constitutionally permissible, Missouri's intrusion upon these fundamental liberties must, at a minimum, bear a reasonable relationship to a legitimate state end. See, e.g., Meyer v. Nebraska, 262 U.S., at 400; Doe v. Bolton, 410 U.S. 179, 194-195, 199 (1973). Missouri asserts that its policy is related to a state interest in the protection of life. In my view, however, it is an effort to define life, rather than to protect it, that is the heart of Missouri's policy. Missouri insists, without regard to Nancy Cruzan's own interests, upon equating her life with the biological persistence of her bodily functions. Nancy Cruzan, it must be remembered, is not now simply incompetent. She is in a persistent vegetative state, and has been so for seven years. The trial court found, and no party contested, that Nancy has no possibility of recovery and no consciousness.

It seems to me that the Court errs insofar as it characterizes this case as involving "judgments about the 'quality' of life that a particular individual may enjoy," ante, at 17. Nancy Cruzan is obviously "alive" in a physiological sense. But for patients like Nancy Cruzan, who have no consciousness and no chance of recovery, there is a serious question as to whether the mere persistence of their bodies is "life" as that word is commonly understood, or as it is used in both the Constitution and the Declaration of Independence.[18] The State's unflagging determination to perpetuate Nancy Cruzan's physical existence is comprehensible only as an effort to define life's meaning, not as an attempt to preserve its sanctity.

This much should be clear from the oddity of Missouri's definition alone. Life, particularly human life, is not commonly thought of as a merely physiological condition or function.[19] Its sanctity is often thought to derive from the impossibility of any such reduction. When people speak of life, they often mean to describe the experiences that comprise a person's history, as when it is said that somebody "led a good life."[20] They may also mean to refer to the practical manifestation of the human spirit, a meaning captured by the familiar observation that somebody "added life" to an assembly. If there is a shared thread among the various opinions on this subject, it may be that life is an activity which is at once the matrix for and an integration of a person's interests. In any event, absent some theological abstraction, the idea of life is not conceived separately from the idea of a living person. Yet, it is by precisely such a separation that Missouri asserts an interest in Nancy Cruzan's life in opposition to Nancy Cruzan's own interests. The resulting definition is uncommon indeed.

The laws punishing homicide, upon which the Court relies, ante, at 16, do not support a contrary inference. Obviously, such laws protect both the life and interests of those who would otherwise be victims. Even laws against suicide presuppose that those inclined to take their own lives have some interest in living, and, indeed, that the depressed people whose lives are preserved may later be thankful for the State's intervention. Likewise, decisions that address the "qualify of life" of incompetent, but conscious, patients rest upon the recognition that these patients have some interest in continuing their lives, even if that interest pales in some eyes when measured against interests in dignity or comfort. Not so here. Contrary to the Court's suggestion, Missouri's protection to life in a form abstracted from the living is not commonplace; it is aberrant.

Nor does Missouri's treatment of Nancy Cruzan find precedent in the various state law cases surveyed by the majority. Despite the Court's assertion that state courts have demonstrated "both similarity and diversity in their approach" to the issue before us, none of the decisions surveyed by the Court interposed an absolute bar to the termination of treatment for a patient in a persistent vegetative state. For example, In re Westchester County Medical Center on behalf of O'Connor, 72 N.Y. 2d 517, 531 N.E. 2d 607 (1988), pertained to an incompetent patient who "was not in a coma or vegetative state. She was conscious, and capable of responding to simple questions or requests sometimes by squeezing the questioner's hand and sometimes verbally." Id., at 524-525, 531 N.E. 2d, at 609-610. Likewise, In re Storar, 52 N.Y. 2d 363, 420 N.E. 2d 64 (1981), involved a conscious patient who was incompetent because "profoundly retarded with a mental age of about 18 months." Id., at 373, 420 N.E. 2d, at 68. When it decided In re Conroy, 98 N.J. 321, 486 A. 2d 1209 (1985), the New Jersey Supreme Court noted that "Ms. Conroy was not brain dead, comatose, or in a chronic vegetative state," 98 N.J., at 337, 486 A. 2d, at 1217, and then distinguished In re Quinlan, 70 N.J. 10, 355 A. 2d 647 (1976), on the ground that Karen Quinlan had been in a "persistent vegetative or comatose state." 98 N.J., at 358-359, 486 A. 2d, at 1228. By contrast, an unbroken stream of cases has authorized procedures for the cessation of treatment of patients in persistent vegetative states.[21] Considered against the background of other cases involving patients in persistent vegetative states, instead of against the broader - and inapt - category of cases involving chronically ill incompetent patients, Missouri's decision in anomolous.

In short, there is no reasonable ground for believing that Nancy Beth Cruzan has any personal interest in the perpetuation of what the State has decided is her life. As I have already suggested, it would be possible to hypothesize such an interest on the basis of theological or philosophical conjecture. But even to posit such a basis for the State's action is to condemn it. It is not within the province of secular government to circumscribe the liberties of the people by regulations designed wholly for the purpose of establishing a sectarian definition of life. See Webster v. Reproductive Services, 492 U.S. _____, _____ - _____ (1989) (STEVENS, J., dissenting).

My disagreement with the court is thus unrelated to its endorsement of the clear and convincing standard of proof for cases of this kind. Indeed, I agree that the controlling facts must be established with unmistakable clarity. The critical question, however, is not how to prove the controlling facts but rather what proven facts should be controlling. In my view, the constitutional answer is clear: the best interests of the individual, especially when buttressed by the interests of all related third parties, must prevail over any general state policy that simply ignores those interests.[22] Indeed, the only apparent secular basis for the State's interest in life is the policy's persuasive impact upon people other than Nancy and her family. Yet, "[a]lthough the State may properly perform a teaching function," and although that teaching may foster respect for the sanctity of life, the State may not pursue its project by infringing constitutionally protected interests for "symbolic effect." Carey v. Population Services International, 431 U.S. 678, 715 (1977) (STEVENS, J., concurring in part and concurring in judgment). The failure of Missouri's policy to heed the interests of a dying individual with respect to matters so private is ample evidence of the policy's illegitimacy.

Only because Missouri has arrogated to itself the power to define life, and only because the Court permits this usurpation, are Nancy Cruzan's life and liberty put into disquieting conflict. If Nancy Cruzan's life were defined by reference to her own interests, so that her life expired when her biological existence ceased serving any of her own interests, then her constitutionally protected interest in freedom from unwanted treatment would not come into conflict with her constitutionally protected interest in life. Conversely, if there were any evidence that Nancy Cruzan herself defined life to encompass every form of biological persistence by a human being, so that the continuation of treatment would serve Nancy's own liberty, then once again there would be no conflict between life and liberty. The opposition of life and liberty in this case are thus not the result of Nancy Cruzan's tragic accident, but are instead the artificial consequence of Missouri's effort, and this Court's willingness, to abstract nancy Cruzan's life form Nancy Cruzan's person.

IV

Both this Court's majority and the state court's majority express great deference to the policy choice made by the state legislature.[23] That deference is, in my view, based upon a severe error in the Court's consitutional logic. The court believes that the liberty interest claimed here on behalf of Nancy Cruzan is peculiarly problematic because "an incompetent person is not able to make an informed and

59

voluntary choice to exercise a hypothetical right to refuse treatment or any other right." Ante, at 15. The impossibility of such an exercise affords the State, according to the Court, some discretion to interpose "a procedural requirement" that effectively compels the continuation of Nancy Cruzan's treatment.

There is, however, nothing "hypothetical" about Nancy Cruzan's constitutionally protected interest in freedom from unwanted treatment, and the difficulties involved in ascertaining what her interests are do not in any way justify the State's decision to oppose her interests with its own. As this case comes to us, the crucial question - and the question addressed by the Court - is not what Nancy Cruzan's interests are, but whether the State must give effect to them. There is certainly nothing novel about the practice of permitting a next friend to assert constitutional rights on behalf of an incompetent patient who is unable to do so. See, e.g., Younberg v. Romeo, 457 U.S. 307, 310 (1982); Whitmore v. Arkansas, 495 U.S. ____, ____ 91990) (slip op. at 11-13). Thus, if Nancy Cruzan's incapacity to "exercise" her rights is to alter the balance between her interests and the State's, there must be some further explanation of how it does so. The Court offers two possibilities, neither of them satisfactory.

The first possibility is that the State's policy favoring life is by its nature less intrusive upon the patient's interest than any alternative. The Court suggests that Missouri's policy "results in a maintenance of the status quo," and is subject to reversal, while a decision to terminate treatment "is not susceptible of correction" because death is irreversible. Ante, at 19. Yet, this explanation begs the question, for it assumes either that the State's policy is consistent with Nancy Cruzan's own interests, or that no damage is done by ignoring her interests. THe first assumption is without basis in the record of this case, and would obviate any need for the State to rely, as it does, upon its own interests rather than upon the patient's. The second assumption is unconscionable. Insofar as Nancy Cruzan has an interest in being remembered for how she lived rather than how she died, the damage done to those memories by the prolongation of her death is irreversible. Insofar as Nancy Cruzan has an interest in the cessation of any pain, the continuation of her pain is irreversible. Insofar as Nancy Cruzan has an interest in a closure to her life consistent with her own beliefs rather than those of the Missouri legislature, the State's imposition of its contrary view is irreversible. To deny the importance of these consequences is in effect to deny that Nancy Cruzan has interests at all, and thereby to deny her personhood in the name of preserving the sanctity of her life.

The second possibility is that the State must be allowed to define the interests of incompetent patients with respect to life-sustaining treatment because there is no procedure capable of determining what those interests are in any particular case. The Court points out various possible "abuses" and inaccuracies that may affect procedures authorizing the termination of treatment. See ante, at 17. The Court correctly notes that in some cases there may be a conflict between the interests of an incompetent patient and the interests of members of her family. A State's procedures must guard against the risk that the survivors' interest are not mistaken for the patient's. Yet, the appointment of the neutral guardian ad litem, coupled with the searching inquiry conducted by the trial judge and the imposition of the clear and convincing standard of proof, all effectively avoided that risk in this case. Why such procedural safeguards should not be adequate to avoid a similar risk in other cases is a question the Court simply ignores.

Indeed, to argue that the mere possibility of error in _any_ case suffices to allow the State's interests to override the particular interests of incompetent individuals in _every_ case, or to argue that the interests of such individuals are unknowable and therefore may be subordinated to the State's concerns, is once again to deny Nancy Cruzan's personhood. The meaning of respect for her personhood, and for that of others who are gravely ill and incapacitated, is, admittedly, not easily defined: choices about life and death are profound ones, not susceptible of resolution by recourse to medical or legal rules. It may be that the best we can do is to ensure that these choices are made by those who will care enough about the patient to investigate her interests with particularity and caution. The Court seems to recognize as much when it cautions against formulating any general or inflexible rule to govern all the cases that might arise in this area of the law. <u>Ante</u>, at 13. The Court's deference to the legislature is, however, itself an inflexible rule, one that the Court is willing to apply in this case even thought he Court's principal ground for deferring to Missouri's legislature are hypothetical circumstances not relevant to Nancy Cruzan's interests.

On either explanation, then, the Court's deference seems ultimately to derive from the premise that chronically incompetent persons have no constitutionally cognizable interests at all, and so are not persons within the meaning of the Constitution. Deference of this sort is patently unconstitutional. It is also dangerous in ways that may not be immediately apparent. Today the State of Missouri has announced its intent to spend several hundred thousand dollars in preserving the life of Nancy Beth Cruzan in order to vindicate its general policy favoring the preservation of human life. Tomorrow, another State equally eager to champion an interest in the "quality of life" might favor a policy designed to ensure quick and comfortable deaths by denying treatment to categories of marginally hopeless cases. If the State in fact has an interest in defining life, and if the State's policy with respect to the termination of life-sustaining treatment commands deference from the judiciary, it is unclear how any resulting conflict between the best interests of the individual and the general policy of the State would be resolved.[24] I believe the Constitution requires that the individual's vital interest in liberty should prevail over the general policy in that case, just as in this.

That a contrary result is readily imaginable under the majority's theory makes manifest that this Court cannot defer to any State policy that drives a theoretical wedge between a person's life, on the one hand, and that person's liberty or happiness, on the other.[25] The consequence of such a theory is to deny the personhood of those whose lives are defined by the State's interests rather than their own. This consequence may be acceptable in theology or in speculative philosophy, see Meyer, 262 U.S., at 401-402, but it is radically inconsistent with the foundation of all legitimate government. Our Constitution presupposes a respect for the personhood of every individual, and nowhere is strict adherence to that principle more essential than in the Judicial Branch. See e.g., Thornburgh v. American College of Obstetricians and Gynecologists, 476 U.S., at 781-782 (STEVENS, J., concurring).

V

In this case, as is no doubt true in many others, the predicament confronted by the healthy members of the Cruzan family merely adds emphasis to the best interests finding made by the trial judge. Each of us has an interest in the kind of memories that will survive after death. To that end, individual decisions are often motivated by their impact on others. A member of the kind of family identified in the trial court's findings in this case would likely have not only a normal interest in minimizing the burden that her own illness imposes on others, but also an interest in having their memories of her filled predominantly with thoughts about her past vitality rather than her current condition. The meaning and completion of her life should be controlled by persons who have her best interests at heart - not by a state legislature concerned only with the "preservation of human life."

The Cruzan family's continuing concern provides a concrete reminder that Nancy Cruzan's interests did not disappear with her vitality or her consciousness. However commendable may be the State's interest in human life, it cannot pursue that interest by appropriating Nancy Cruzan's life as a symbol for its own purposes. Lives do not exist in abstraction from persons, and to pretend otherwise is not to honor but to desecrate the State's responsibility for protecting life. A State that seeks to demonstrate its commitment to life may do so by aiding those who are actively struggling for life and health. In this endeavor, unfortunately, no State can lack for opportunities: there can be no need to make an example of tragic cases like that of Nancy Cruzan.

I respectfully dissent.

[1] The State Supreme Court, adopting much of the trial court's findings, described Nancy Cruzan's medical condition as follows:
"... (1) [H]er respiration and circulation are not artificially maintained and are within the normal limits of a thirty-year-old female; (2) she is oblivious to her environment except for reflexive responses to sound and perhaps painful stimuli; (3) she suffered anoxia of the brain resulting in a massive enlargement of the ventricles filling with cerebrospinal fluid in the area where the brain has degenerated and [her] cerebral cortical atrophy is irreversible, permanent, progressive and ongoing; (4) her highest cognitive brain function is exhibited by her grimacing perhaps in recognition of ordinarily painful stimuli, indicating the experience of pain and apparent response to sound; (5) she is a spastic quadriplegic; (6) her four extremities are contracted with irreversible muscular and tendon damage to all extremities; (7) she has no cognitive or reflexive ability to swallow food or water to maintain her daily essential needs and ... she will never recover her ability to swallow sufficient [sic] to satisfy her needs. In sum, Nancy is diagnosed as in a persistent vegetative state. She is not dead. She is not terminally ill. Medical experts testified that she could live another thirty years." Cruzan v. Harmon, 760 S.W. 2d 408, 411 (Mo. 1989) (en banc) (quotations omitted; footnote omitted).

In observing that Cruzan was not dead, the court referred to the following Missouri statute:
"For all legal purposes, the occurrence of human death shall be determined in accordance with the usual and customary standards of medical practice, provided that death shall not be determined to have occurred unless the following minimal conditions have been met:
    "(1) When respiration and circulation are not artificially maintained, there is an irreversible cessation of spontaneous respiration and circulation; or
    "(2) When respiration and circulation are artificially maintained, and there is total and irreversible cessation of all brain function, including the brain stem and that such determination is made by a licensed physician." Mo. Rev. Stat. section 194.005 (1986).

Since Cruzan's respiration and circulation were not being artificially maintained, she obviously fit within the first proviso of the statute.

    Dr. Fred Plum, the creator of the term "persistent vegetative state" and a renowned expert on the subject, has described the "vegetative state" in the following terms:
"`Vegetative state describes a body which is functioning entirely in terms of its internal controls. It maintains temperature. It maintains heart beat and pulmonary ventilation. It maintains digestive activity. It maintains reflex activity of muscles and nerves for low level conditioned responses. But there is no behavioral evidence of either self-awareness of awareness or the surroundings in a learned manner.'" In re Jobes, 108 N.J. 394, 403, 529 A. 2d 434, 438 (1987). See also Brief for American Medical Association et al., as Amici

<u>Curiae</u>, 6 ("The persistent vegetative state can best be understood as one of the conditions in which patients have suffered a loss of consciousness").

[2] See generally Karnezis, Patient's Right to Refuse Treatment Allegedly Necessary to Sustain Life, 93 A.L.R. 3d 67 (1979) (collecting cases); Cantor, A Patient's Decision to Decline Life-Saving Medical Treatment: Bodily Integrity Versus the Preservation of Life, 26 Rutgers L. Rev. 228, 229, and n. 5 (1973) (noting paucity of cases).

[3] See Chapman, The Uniform Rights of the Terminally Ill Act: Too Little, Too Late?, 42 Ark. L. Rev. 319, 324, n. 15 (1989); see also F. Rozovsky, Consent to Treatment, A Practical Guide 415-423 (2d ed. 1984).

[4] In a later trilogy of cases, the New Jersey Supreme Court stressed that the analytic framework adopted in <u>Conroy</u> was limited to elderly, incompetent patients with shortened life expectancies, and established alternative approaches to deal with a different set of situations. See <u>In re Farrell</u>, 108 N.J. 335, 529 A. 2d 404 (1987) (37-year-old competent mother with terminal illness had right to removal of respirator based on common law and constitutional principles which overrode competing state interests); <u>In re Peter</u>, 108 N.J. 365, 529 A. 2d 419 (1987) (65-year-old woman in persistent vegetative state had right to removal of nasogastric feeding tube - under <u>Conroy</u> subjective test, power of attorney and hearsay testimony constituted clear and convincing proof of patient's intent to have treatment withdrawn); <u>In re Jobes</u>, 108 N.J. 394, 529 A. 2d 434 (1987) (31-year-old woman in persistent vegetative state entitled to removal of jejunostomy feeding tube - even though hearsay testimony regarding patient's intent insufficient to meet clear an convincing standard of proof, under <u>Quinlan</u>, family or close friends entitled to make a substituted judgment for patient).

[5] The <u>Drabick</u> court drew support for its analysis from earlier, influential decisions rendered by California courts of appeal. See <u>Bouvia v. Superior Court</u>, 179 Cal. App. 3d 1127, 225 Cal. Rptr. 297 (1986) (competent 28-year-old quadriplegic had right to removal of nasogastric feeding tube inserted against her will); <u>Bartling v. Superior Court</u>, 163 Cal. App. 3d 186, 209 Cal. Rptr. 220 (1984) (competent 70-year-old, seriously-ill man had right to the removal of respirator); <u>Barber v. Superior Court</u>, 147 Cal. App. 3d 1006, 195 Cal. Rptr. 484 (1983) (physicians could not be prosecuted for homicide on account of removing respirator and intravenous feeding tubes of patient in persistent vegetative state).

[6] Besides the Missouri Supreme Court in <u>Cruzan</u> and the courts in <u>McConnell</u>, <u>Longeway</u>, <u>Drabick</u>, <u>Bouvia</u>, <u>Barber</u>, <u>O'Connor</u>, <u>Conroy</u>, <u>Jobes</u>, and <u>Peter</u>, <u>supra</u>, appellate courts of at least four other States and one Federal District Court have specifically considered and discussed the issue of withholding or withdrawing artificial nutrition and hydration from incompetent individuals. See <u>Gray v. Romeo</u>, 697 F. Supp. 580 (RI 1988); <u>In re Gardner</u>, 534 A. 2d 947 (Me. 1987); <u>In re Grant</u>, 109 Wash. 2d 545, 747 P. 2d 445 (Wash. 1987); <u>Brophy v. New England Sinai Hospital, Inc.</u>, 398 Mass. 417, 497 N.E. 2d 626 (1986);

Corbett v. D'Alessandro, 487 So. 2d 368 (Fla. App. 1986). All of these courts permitted or would permit the termination of such measures based on rights grounded in the common law, or in the State or Federal Constitution.

[7] Although many state courts have held that a right to refuse treatment is encompassed by a generalized constitutional right of privacy, we have never so held. We believe this issue is more properly analyzed in terms of a Fourteenth Amendment liberty interest. See Bowers v. Hardwick, 478 U.S. 186, 194-195 (1986).

[8] See Smith, All's Well That Ends Well: Toward a Policy of Assisted Rational Suicide or Merely Enlightened Self-Determination:, 22 U.C. Davis L. Rev. 275, 290-291, n. 106 (1989) (compiling statutes).

[9] Since Cruzan was a patient at a state hospital when this litigation commences, the State has been involved as an adversary from the beginning. However, it can be expected that many of these types of disputes will arise in private institutions, where a guardian ad litem or similar party will have been appointed as the sole representative of the incompetent individual in the litigation. In such cases, a guardian may act in entire good faith, and yet not maintain a position truly adversarial to that of the family. Indeed, as noted by the court below, "[t]he guardian ad litem [in this case] finds himself in the predicament of believing that it is in Nancy's `best interest to have the tube feeding discontinued,' but `feeling that an appeal should be made because our responsibility to her as attorneys and guardians ad litem was to pursue this matter to the highest court in the state in view of the fact that this is a case of first impression in the State of Missouri.'" 760 S.W. 2d, at 410, n. 1. Cruzan's guardian ad litem has also filed a brief in this Court urging reversal of the Missouri Supreme Court's decision. None of this is intended to suggest that the guardian acted the least bit improperly in this proceeding. It is only meant to illustrate the limits which may obtain on the adversarial nature of this type of litigation.

[10] We recognize that these cases involved instances where the government sought to take action against an individual. See Price Waterhouse v. Hopkins, 4990 U.S. _____, _____ (1989) (plurality opinion). Here, by contrast, the government seeks to protect the interests of an individual, as well as its own institutional interests, in life. We do not see any reason why important individual interests should be afforded less protection simply because the government finds itself in the position of defending them. "[W]e find it significant that ... the defendant rather than the plaintiff" seeks the clear and convincing standard of proof - "suggesting that this standard ordinarily serves as a shield rather than ... a sword." Id., at _____. That it is the government that has picked up the shield should be of no moment.

[11] The clear and convincing standard of proof has been variously defined in this context as "proof sufficient to persuade the trier of fact that the patient held a firm and settled commitment to the termination of life supports under the circumstances like those presented," In re Westchester County Medical Center on behalf of

O'Connor, 72 N.Y. 2d 517, 531, N.E. 2d 607, 613 (1988) (O'Connor), and as evidence which "produces in the mind of the trier of fact a firm belief or conviction as to the truth of the allegations sought to be established, evidence so clear, direct and weighty and convincing as to enable [the factfinder] to come to a clear conviction, without hesitancy, of the truth of the precise facts in issue." In re Jobes, 108 N.J., at 407-408, 529 A. 2d, at 441 (quotation omitted). In both of these cases the evidence of the patient's intent to refuse medical treatment was arguably stronger that that presented here. The New York Court of Appeals and the Supreme court of New Jersey, respectively, held that the proof failed to meet a clear and convincing threshold. See O'Connor, supra, at 526-534, 531 N.E. 2d, at 610-615; Jobes, supra, at 442-443.

[12] We are not faced in this case with the question of whether a State might be required to defer to the decision of a surrogate if competent and probative evidence established that the patient herself had expressed a desire that the decision to terminate life-sustaining treatment be made for her by that individual.

Petitioners also adumbrate in their brief a claim based on the Equal Protection Clause of the Fourteenth Amendment to the effect that Missouri has impermissibly treated incompetent patients differently from competent ones, citing the statement in Cleburne v. Cleburne Living Center, Inc., 473 U.S. 432, 439 (1985), that the clause is "essentially a direction that all persons similarly situated should be treated alike." The differences between the choice may by a competent person to refuse medical treatment, and the choice made for an incompetent person by someone else to refuse medical treatment, are so obviously different that the State is warranted in establishing rigorous procedures for the latter class of cases which do not apply to the former class.

(Editor's Note - The folowing are the footnotes to the concurring opinion of Justice O'Connor.)

[1] See 2 President's commission for the Study of Ethical Problems in Medicine and Biomedical and Behavioral Research, Making Health care Decision 241-242 (1982) (36% of those surveyed gave instructions regarding how they would like to be treated it they ever became too sick to make decisions; 23% put those instruction in writing) (Lou Harris Poll, September 1982); American Medical Association Surveys of Physician and Public Opinion on Health Care Issues 29-30 (1988) (56% of those surveyed had told family members their wishes concerning the use of life-sustaining treatment if they entered an irreversible coma; 15% had filled out a living will specifying those wishes).

[2] At least 13 states and the District of Columbia have durable power of attorney statutes expressly authorizing the appointment of proxies for making health care decisions. See Alaska State. Ann. Section 13.26.335, 13.26.344(1) (Supp. 1989); Cal Civ. Code Section 2500 (Supp. 1990); D.C. Code Section 21-2205 (1989); Idaho Code Section 39-4505 (Supp. 1989); Ill. Rev. Stat., ch. 1101/2, Section 804-1-804-12 (Supp. 1988); Kan. Stat. Ann. Section 58-625 (Supp. 1989); Me. Rev. Stat. Ann., Titl. 18-A, Section 5-501 (Supp. 1989); Nev. Rev. Stat. Section

449.800 (Supp. 1989); Ohio Rev. Code Ann. Section 1337.11 et seq. (Supp. 1989); Ore. Rev. Stat. Section 127.510 (1989); Pa. Stat. Ann., Titl 20, Section 5603(h) (Purdon Supp. 1989); R.I. Gen. Laws Sections 23-4.10-1 et seq. (1989); Tex Rev. Civ. Stat. Ann. Section 4590h-1 (Vernon Supp. 1990); Vt. Stat. Ann., Tit. 14, Section 3451 et seq. (1989).

[3] All 50 states and the District of Columbia have general durable power of attorney statutes. See Ala. Code Section 26-1-2 (1986); Alaska Stat. Ann. Sections 13-26-350 to 13-26-356 (Supp. 1989); Ariz. Rev. Stat. Ann. Section 14-5501 (1975); Ark. Code Ann. Sections 28-68-201 to 28-68-203 (1987); Cal. Civ. Code Ann. Section 2400 (West Supp. 1990); Colo. Rev. Stat. Section 15-14-501 et seq. (1987); Conn. Gen. Stat. Section 45-69o (Supp. 1989); Del. Code Ann., Tit. 12, Section 4901-4905 (1987); D.C. Code Section 21-2081 et. seq. (1989); Fla. Stat. Section 709.08 (1989); Ga. Code Ann. Section 10-6-46 (1989); Haw. Rev. Stat. Sections 551D-1 to 551D-7 (Supp. 1989). Idaho Code Section 15-5-501 et seq. (Supp. 1989). Ill, rev. Stat., ch. 1101/2, Section 802-6 (1987); Ind. Code Sections 30-2-11-1 to 30-2-11-7 (1988); Iowa Code Section 633.705 (Supp. 1989); Kan. Stat. Ann. Section 58-610 (1983); Ky. Rev. Stat. Ann. Sectin 386.093 (Baldwin 1983); La. Civ. Code Ann. Section 3027 (West Supp. 1990); Me. Rev. Stat. Ann., Tit. 18-A, Section 5-501 et seq. (Supp. 1989); Md. Est. & Trusts Code Ann. Section 13-601-13 to 602 (1974) (as interpreted by the Attorney General, see 73 Op. Md. Atty. Gen. No. 88-046 (Oct. 17, 1988)); Mass. Gen. Laws Sections 201B:a to 201B:7 (1988); Mich. Compt. Laws Section 700-495, 70000000.497 (1980); Minn. Stat. Section 523.01 et seq. (1988); Miss. Code Ann. Section 87-3-13 (Supp. 1989). Mo. Rev. Stat. Section 404.700 (Supp. 1990); Mont. Code Ann. Sections 72-5-501 to 72-5-502 (1989); Neb. Rev. Stat. Sections 30-2664 to 30-2672, 30-2667 (1985); Nev. Rev. Stat. Section 111.460 et seq. (1986); N.H. Rev. Stat. Ann. Section 506:6 et seq. (Supp. 1989); N.J. Stat. Ann. Section 46:2B-8 (1989); N.M. Stat. Ann. Section 45-5-501 et seq. (1989); N.Y. Gen. Oblig. Law Section 5-1602 (McKinney 1989); N.C. Gen. Stat. Section 32A-1 et seq. 91987); N.D. Cent. Code Sections 30.1-30 to 01-30.1-30-05 (Supp. 1989); Ohio Rev. Code Ann. Section 1337.09 (SUpp. 1989); Okla. Stat., Tit. 58, Sections 1071-1077 (Supp. 1989). Ore. Rev. Stat. Section 127.005 (1989). Pa. Stat. Ann., Tit. 20, Section 5601 et seq., 5602(a)(9) (Purdon Supp. 1989); R.I. Gen. LAws Section 34-22-6.1 (1984); S.C. Code Sections 62-5-501 to 62-5-502 (1987); S.D. Codified Laws Section 59-7-2.1 (1978); Tenn. Code Ann. Section 34-6-101 et seq. (1984); Tex Prob. Code Ann. Section 36A (Supp. 1990); Utah Code Ann. Section 75-5-501 et seq. (1978); Vt. Stat. Ann., Tit. 14, Section 3051 et seq. (1989). W. Va. Code Section 39-4-1 et seq. (Supp. 1989); Wis. Sta. Section 243.07 (1987-1988); (as interpreted by the Attorney General, see Wis. Op. Atty. Gen. 35-88 91988), Wyo. Stat. Section 3-5-101 e seq. (Supp. 1985).

[4] Thirteen states have living will statutes authorizing the appointment of healthcare proxies. See Ark. Code Ann. Section 20-17-202 (Supp. 1989); Del. Code Ann., Tit. 16, Section 2502 (1983); Fla. Stat. Section 765.05(2) (1989); Idaho Code Section 39-4504 (Supp. 1989); Ind. Code Section 16-8-11-14(g)(2) (1988); Iowa Code Section 144A.7(1)(a) (1989); La. Civ. Code Ann., Art. 40:1299.58.1, 40:1299.58.3(C) (West Supp. 1990); Minn. Stat. Section 145B.01 et seq. (Supp. 1989); Texas Health

& Safety Code Ann. Section 672/003(d) (Supp. 1990); Utah Code Ann. Section 75-2-1105, 75-2-1106 (Supp. 1989); Va. Code Section 54.1-2986(2) (1988); 1987 Wash. Laws, ch. 162 Section 1(1)(b); Wyo. Stat. Section 35-22-102 (1988).

(Editor's Note - The following are the footnotes to the dissenting opinion of Justice Brennen, Marshall, and Blackmun.)

[1] Rasmussen v. Fleming, 154 Ariz. 207, 211, 741 P. 2d 674, 678 (1987) (en banc).

[2] Vegetative state patients may react reflexively to sounds, movements and normally painful stimuli, but they do not feel any pain or sense anybody or anything. Vegetative state patients may appear awake but are completely unaware. See Cranford, The Persistent Vegetative State: The Medical Reality, 18 Hastings Ctr. Rep. 27, 28, 31 (1988).

[3] See President's Commission for the Study of Ethical Problems in Medicine and Biomedical and Behavioral Research, Deciding to Forego Life Sustaining Treatment 15, n. 1, and 17-18 (1983) (hereafter President's Commission).

[4] See Lipton, Do-Not-Resuscitate Decisions in a Community Hospital: Incidence, Implications and Outcomes, 256 JAMA 1164, 1168 (1986).

[5] See e.g., Canterbury v. Spence, 150 U.S. App. D.C. 263, 271, 464 F. 2d 772, 780, cert. denied, 409 U.S. 1064 (1972) ("The root premise" of informed consent "is the concept, fundamental in American jurisprudence, that `[e]very human being of adult years and sound mind has a right to determine what shall be done with his own body'".) (quoting Schloendorff v. Society of New York Hospital, 211 N.Y. 125, 129-130, 105 N.E. 92, 93 (1914) (Cardozo, J.)). See generally Washington v. Harper, 494 U.S. ____, ____ (1990) (STEVENS J., dissenting) (slip op., at 5) ("There is no doubt ... that a competent individual's right to refuse [psychotropic] medication is a fundamental liberty interest deserving the highest order of protection").

[6] Under traditional tort law, exceptions have been found only to protect dependent children. See Cruzan v. Harmon, 760 S.W. 2d 408, 422, n. 17 (Mo. 1988) (citing cases where Missouri courts have ordered blood transfusions for children over the religious objection of parents); see also Winthrop University Hospital v. Hess, 128 Misc. 2d 804, 490 N.Y.S. 2d 996 (Sup. Ct. Nassau Co. 1985) (court ordered blood transfusion for religious objector because she was the mother of an infant and had explained that her objection was to the signing of the consent, not the transfusion itself); Application of President & Directors of Georgetown College, Inc., 118 U.S. App. D.C. 80, 88, 331 F. 2d 1000, 1008, cert. denied, 377 U.S. 978 (1964) (blood transfusion ordered for mother of infant). Cf. In re Estate of Brooks 32, Ill, 2d 361, 373, 205 N.E. 2d 435, 441-442 (1965) (finding that lower court erred in ordering a blood transfusion for a woman - whose children were grown - and concluding: "Even though we may consider apellant's beliefs unwise, foolish or ridiculous,in the absence of an overriding danger to society we may not permit interference therewith in the form of a

conservatorship established in the waning hours of her life for the sole purpose of compelling her to accept medical treatment forbidden by her religious principles, and previously refused by her with full knowledge of the probable consequences").

[7] The Missouri court appears to be alone among state courts to suggest otherwise, 760 S.W. 2d, at 419 and 423, although the court did not rely on a distinction between artificial feeding and other forms of medical treatment. Id., at 423. See, e.g., Delio v. Westchester County Medical Center, 129 App. Div. 2d 1, 19, 516 N.Y.S. 2d 677, 689 (1987) ("review of the decisions in other jurisdictions ... failed to uncover a single case in which a court confronted with an application to discontinue feeding by artificial means has evaluated medical procedures to provide nutrition and hydration differently from other types of life-sustaining procedures").

[8] While brain stem cells can survive 15 to 20 minutes without oxygen, cells in the cerebral hemispheres are destroyed if they are deprived of oxygen for as few as 4 to 6 minutes. See Cranford & Smith, Some Critical Distinctions Between Brain Death and the Persistent Vegetative State, 6 Ethics Sci. & Med. 199, 203 (1979). It is estimated that Nancy's brain was deprived of oxygen from 12 to 14 minutes. See ante, at 2. Out of the 100,000 patients who, like Nancy, have fallen into persistive vegetative states in the past 20 years due to loss of oxygen to the brain, there have been only three even partial recoveries documented in the medical literature. Brief for American Medical Association et al. as Amici Curiae 11-12. The longest any person has ever been in a persistent vegetative state and recovered was 22 months. See Snyder, Cranford, Rubens, Bundlie, & Rockswold, Delayed Recovery from Postanoxic Persistent Vegetative State, 15 Annals Neurol. 156 (1983). Nancy has been in this state for seven years.

[9] The American Academy of Neurology offers three independent bases on which the medical profession rests these neurological conclusions:
"First, direct clinical experience with these patients demonstrates that there is no behavioral indication of nay awareness of pain or suffering.
"Second, in all persistent vegetative state patients studied to date, postmortem examination reveals overwhelming bilateral damage to the cerebral hemispheres to a degree incompatible with consciousness.
"Third, recent data utilizing positron emission tomography indicates that the metabolic rate for glucose in the cerebral cortex is greatly reduced in persistent vegetative state patients, to a degree incompatible with consciousness." Position of the American Academy of Neurology on Certain Aspects of the Care and Management of the Persistent Vegetative State patient, 39 Neurology 125 (Jan. 1989).

[10] Nancy Cruzan, for instance, is totally and permanently disabled. All four of her limbs are severely contracted; her fingernails cut into her wrists. App. to Pet. for Cert. A93. She is incontinent of bowel and bladder. The most intimate aspects of her existence are exposed to and controlled by strangers. Brief for Respondent Guardian Ad Litem 2. Her family is convinced that Nancy would find this state degrading. See n. 20, infra.

[11] What general information exists about what most people would choose or would prefer to have chosen for them under these circumstances also indicates the importance of ensuring a means for now-incompetent patients to exercise their right to avoid unwanted medical treatment. A 1988 poll conducted by the American Medical Association found that 80% of those surveyed favored withdrawal of life support systems from hopelessly ill or irreversibly comatose patients if they or their families requested it. New York Times, June 5, 1988, p. 14, col. 4 (citing American Medical News, June 3, 1988, p. 9, col. 1). Another 1988 poll conducted by the Colorado University Graduate School of Public Affairs showed that 85% of those questioned would not want to have their own lives maintained with artificial nutrition and hydration if they became permanently unconscious. The Coloradoan, Sept. 29, 1988, p. 1.

Such attitudes have been translated into considerable political action. Since 1976, 40 States and the District of Columbia have enacted natural death acts, expressly providing for self-determination under some or all of these situations. See Brief for Society for the Right to Die, Inc. as Amicus Curiae 8; Weiner, Privacy, Family, and Medical Decision Making for Persistent Vegetative Patients, 11 Cardozo L. Rev. 713, 720 (1990) Thirteen States and the District of Columbia have enacted statutes authorizing the appointment of proxies for making health care decisions. See ante, at 4, n. 2 (O'CONNOR, J., concurring).

[12] See Jacobson v. Massachusetts, 197 U.S. 11, 26-27 (1905) (upholding a Massachusetts law imposing fines or imprisonment on those refusing to be vaccinated as "of paramount necessity" to that State's fight against a smallpox epidemic).

[13] Were such interests at stake, however, I would find that the Due Process Clause places limits on what invasive medical procedures could be forced on an unwilling comatose patient in pursuit of the interests of a third party. If Missouri were correct that its interests outweigh Nancy's interest in avoiding medical procedures as long as she is free of pain and physical discomfort, see 760 S.W. 2d, at 424, it is not apparent why a State could not choose to remove one of her kidneys without consent on the ground that society would be better off if the recipient of that kidney were saved from renal poisoning. Nancy cannot feel surgical pain. See n. 2, supra. Nor would removal of one kidney be expected to shorten her life expectancy. See The American Medical Association Family Medical Guide 506 (J. Kunz ed. 1982). Patches of her skin could also be removed to provide grafts for burn victims, and scrapings of bone marrow to provide grafts for someone with leukemia. Perhaps the State could lawfully remove more vital organs for transplanting into others who would then be cured of their ailments, provided the State placed Nancy on some other life-support equipment to replace the lost function. Indeed, why could the State not perform medical experiments on her body, experiments that might save countless lives, and would cause her no greater burden than she already bears by being fed through the gastrostomy tube? This would be too brave a new world for me and, I submit, for our Constitution.

[14] The Missouri Supreme Court reviewed the state interests that had been identified by other courts as potentially relevant - prevention of homicide and suicide, protection of interests of innocent third parties, maintenance of the ethical integrity of the medical profession, and preservation of life - and concluded that: "In this case, only the state's interest in the preservation of life is implicated." 760 S.W. 2d, at 419.

[15] In any event, the State interest identified by the Missouri Supreme Court - a comprehensive and "unqualified" interest in preserving life, id., at 420, 424 - is not even well supported by that State's own enactments. In the first place, Missouri has no law requiring every person to procure any needed medical care nor a state health insurance program to underwrite such care. Id., at 429 (Blackmar, J., dissenting). Second, as the state court admitted, Missouri has a living will statute which specifically "allows and encourages the pre-planned termination of life." Ibid.; see Mo. Rev. Stat. Section 459.015(a) (1986). The fact that Missouri actively provides for its citizens to choose a natural death under certain circumstances suggests that the State's interest in life is not so unqualified as the court below suggests. It is true that this particular statute does not apply to nonterminal patients and does not include artificial nutrition and hydration as one of the measure that may be declined. Nonetheless, Missouri has also not chosen to require court review of every decision to withhold or withdraw life-support made on behalf of an incompetent patient. Such decisions are made every day, without state participation. See 760 S.W. 2d. at 428 (Blackmar, J., dissenting).

In addition, precisely what implication can be drawn from the statute's limitations is unclear given the inclusion of a series of "interpretive" provision in the Act. The first such provision explains that the Act is to be interpreted consistently with the following: "Each person has the primary right to request or refuse medical treatment subject to the state's interest in protecting innocent third parties, preventing homicide and suicide and preserving good ethical standards in the medical profession." Mo. Rev. Stat. Section 459.055(1) (1986). The second of these subsections explains that the Act's provisions are cumulative and not intended to increase or decrease the right of a patient to make decisions or lawfully effect the withholding or withdrawal of medical care. Section 459.055(2). The third subsection provides that "no presumption concerning the intention of an individual who has not executed a declaration to consent to the use or withholding of medical procedures" shall be created. Section 459.055(3).

Thus, even if it were conceivable that a State could assert an interest sufficiently compelling to overcome Nancy Cruzan's constitutional right, Missouri law demonstrates a more modest interest at best. See generally Capital Cities Cable, Inc. v. Crisp, 467 U.S. 691, 715 (1984) (finding that state regulations narrow in scope indicated that State had only a moderate interest in its professed goal).

[16] See Colorado v. New Mexico, 467 U.S. 310 (1984) (requiring clear and convincing evidence before one State is permitted to divert water from another to accommodate society's interests in stabile property rights and efficient use of resources); New York v. New Jersey, 256 U.S. 296

71

(1921) (promoting federalism by requiring clear and convincing evidence before using Court's power to control the conduct of one State at the behest of another); Maxwell Land - Grant Case, 121 U.S. 324 (1887) (requiring clear, unequivocal, and convincing evidence to set aside, annual or correct a patent or other title to property issued by the Government in order to secure settled expectations concerning property rights); Marcum v. Zaring, 406 P. 2d 970 (Okla. 1965) (promoting stability of marriage by requiring clear and convincing evidence to prove its invalidity); Stevenson v. Stein, 412 Pa. 478, 195 A. 2d 268 (1963) (promoting settled expectations concerning property rights by requiring clear and convincing evidence to prove adverse possession).

[17] The majority's definition of the "status quo," of course, begs the question. Artificial delivery of nutrition and hydration represents the "status quo" only if the State has chosen to permit doctors and hospitals to keep a patient on life-support systems over the protests of his family or guardian. The "status quo" absent that state interference would be the natural result of his accident or illness (and the family's decision). The majority's definition of status quo, however, is "to a large extent a predictable, yet accidental confluence of technology, psyche, and inertia. The general citizenry ... never said that it favored the creation of coma wards where permanently unconscious patients would be tended for years and years. Nor did the populace as a whole authorize the preeminence of doctors over families in making treatment decisions for incompetent patients." Rhoden, Litigating Life and Death, 102 Harv. L. Rev. 375, 433-434 (1988).

[18] For Nancy Cruzan, no such cure or improvement is in view. So much of her brain has deteriorated and been replaced by fluid, see App. to Pet. for Cert. A94, that apparently the only medical advance that could restore consciousness to her body would be a brain transplant. Cf. n. 22, infra.

[19] The trial court had relied on the testimony of Athena Comer, a long-time friend, co-worker and a housemate for several months, as sufficient to show that Nancy Cruzan would wish to be free of medical treatment under her present circumstances. App. to Pet. for Cert. A94. Ms. Comer described a conversation she and Nancy had while living together, concerning Ms. Comer's sister who had become ill suddenly and died during the night. The Comer family had been told that if she had lived through the night, she would have been in a vegetative state. Nancy had lost a grandmother a few months before. Ms. Comer testified that: "Nancy said she would never want to live [as a vegetative state] because if she couldn't be normal or even, you know, like half way, and do things for yourself, because Nancy always did, that she didn't want to live ... and we talked about it a lot." Tr. 388-389. She said "several times" that "she wouldn't want to live that way because if she was going to live, she wanted to be able to live, not to just lay in a bed and not be able to move because you can't do anything for yourself." Id., at 390, 396. "[S]he said that she hoped that [all the] people in her family knew that she wouldn't want to live [as a vegetable] because she knew it was usually up to the family whether you lived that way or not." Id., at 399.

The conversation took place approximately a year before Nancy's accident and was described by Ms. Comer as a "very serious" conversation that continued for approximately half an hour without interruption. Id., at 390. The Missouri Supreme Court dismissed Nancy's statement as "unreliable" on the ground that it was an informally expressed reaction to other people's medical conditions. 760 S.W. 2d, at 424.

The Missouri Supreme Court did not refer to other evidence of Nancy's wishes or explain why it was rejected. Nancy's sister Christy, to whom she was very close, testified that she and Nancy had had two very serious conversations about a year and a half before the accident. A day or two after their niece was stillborn (but would have been badly damaged if she had lived), Nancy had said that maybe it was part of a "greater plan" that the baby had been stillborn and did not have to face "the possible life of mere existence." Tr. 537. A month later, after their grandmother had died after a long battle with heart problems, Nancy said that "it was better for my grandmother not to be kind of brought back and forth [by] medical [treatment], brought back from a critical near point of death. ... id., at 541.

[20] Nancy's sister Christy, Nancy's mother, and another of Nancy's friends testified that Nancy would want to discontinue the hydration and nutrition. Christy said that "Nancy would be horrified at the state she is in." Id., at 535. She would also "want to take that burden away from [her family]. Id., at 544. Based on "a lifetime of experience [I know Nancy's wishes] are to discontinue the hydration and the nutrition." id., at 542. Nancy's mother testified: "Nancy would not want to be like she is now. [I]f it were me up there or Christy or any of us, she would be doing for us what we are trying to do for her. I know she would, ... as her mother." id., at 526.

[21] Surveys show that the overwhelming majority of Americans have not executed such written instruction. See Emmanuel & Emmanuel, The Medical Directive: A New Comprehensive Advance Care Document, 261 JAMA 3288 (1989) (only 9% of Americans execute advance directives about how they would wish treatment decisions to be handled if they became incompetent); American Medical Association Surveys of Physician and Public Opinion on health care Issues 29-30 91988) (only 15% of those surveyed had executed living wills); 2 President's Commission for the Study of Ethical Problems in Medicine and Biomedical and Behavioral Research, Making Health care Decisions 241-242 (1982) (23% of those surveyed said that they had put treatment instructions in writing).

[22] New York is the only State besides Missouri to deny a request to terminate life support on the ground that clear and convincing evidence of prior, expressed intent was absent, although New York did so in the context of very different situations. Mrs. O'Connor, the subject of In re O'Connor, had several times expressed her desire not to be placed on life-support if she were not going to be able to care for herself. However, both of here daughters testified that they did not know whether their mother would want to decline artificial nutrition and hydration under her present circumstances. Cf. n. 13, supra. Moreover, despite damage from several strokes, Mrs. O'Connor was conscious and capable of responding to simple questions and requests and the medical testimony suggested she might improve to some extent. Cf. supra, at 1. The New York court of Appeals also denied permission to terminate blood transfusions for a severely retarded man with terminal cancer because

there was no evidence of a treatment choice made by the man when competent, as he had never been competent. See In re Storar, 52 N.Y. 2d 363, 420 N.E. 2d 64, cert. denied, 454 U.S. 858 (1981). Again, the court relied on evidence that the man was conscious, functioning in the way he always had, and that the transfusions did not cause him substantial pain (although it was clear he did not like them).

[23] Only in the exceedingly rare case where the State cannot find any family member or friend who can be trusted to endeavor genuinely to make the treatment choice the patient would have made does the State become the legitimate surrogate decisionmaker.

[24] Fadiman, The Liberation of Lolly and Gronky, Life Magazine, Dec. 1986, p. 72 (quoting medical ethicist Joseph Fletcher).

(Editor's Note - The following are the footnotes to the dissenting opinion of Justice Stevens.)

[1] It is stated in the Declaration of Independence that:
"We hold these truths to be self-evident, that all men are created equal, that they are endowed by their Creator with certain unalienable Rights, that among these are Life, Liberty and the pursuit of Happiness. - That to secure these rights, Governments are instituted among Men, deriving their just powers from the consent of the governed, - That whenever any Form of Government becomes destructive of these ends, it is the Right of the People to alter or to abolish it, and to institute new Government, laying its foundation on such principles and organizing its powers in such form, as to them shall seem most likely to effect their Safety and Happiness.

[2] The trial court found as follows on the basis of "clear and convincing evidence:"
"1. That her respiration and circulation are not artificially maintained and within essentially normal limits for a 30 year old female with vital signs recently reported as BP 130/80; pulse 78 and regular; respiration spontaneous at 16 to 18 per minute.
"2. That she is oblivious to her environment except for reflexive responses to sound and perhaps to painful stimuli.
"3. That she has suffered anoxia of the brain resulting in massive enlargement of the ventricles filling with cerebrospinal fluid in the area where the brain has degenerated. This cerebral cortical atrophy is irreversible, permanent, progressive and ongoing.
"4. That her highest cognitive brain function is exhibited by her grimacing perhaps in recognition of ordinarily painful stimuli, indicating the experience of pain and her apparent response to sound.
"5. That she is spastic quadriplegic.
"6. That she has contractures of her four extremities which are slowly progressive with irreversible muscular and tendon damage to all extremities.
"7. That she has no cognitive or reflexive ability to swallow food or water to maintain her daily essential needs. That she will never recover her ability to swallow sufficient to satisfy her needs." App. to Pet. for Cert., at A94-A95.

[3] "The only economic considerations in this case rest with Respondent's employer, the State of Missouri, which is bearing the entire cost of care. Our ward is an adult without financial resources other than Social Security whose not inconsiderable medical insurance has been exhausted since January 1986." Id., at A96.

[4] "In this case there are no innocent third parties requiring state protection, neither homicide nor suicide will be committed and the consensus of the medical witnesses indicated concerns personal to themselves or the legal consequences of such actions rather than any objections that good ethical standards of the profession would be breached if the nutrition and hydration were withdrawn the same as any other artificial death prolonging procedures the statute specifically authorizes." Id., at A98.

[5] "Nancy's present unresponsive and hopeless existence is not the will of the Supreme Ruler but of man's will to forcefully feed her when she herself cannot swallow thus fueling respiratory and circulatory pumps to no cognitive purpose for her except sound and perhaps pain." Id., at A97.

[6] "Appellant guardian ad litem advised this court:
    "`We informed the [trial] court that we felt it was in Nancy Cruzan's best interests to have the tube feeding discontinued. We now find ourselves in the position of appealing from a judgment we basically agree with.'" Cruzan v. Harmon, 760 S.W. 2d 408, 435 (Mo. 1988) (Higgins, J., dissenting).

[7] "Four state interests have been identified: preservation of life, prevention of homicide and suicide, the protection of interests of innocent third parties and the maintenance of the ethical integrity of the medical profession. See Section 459.055(1), RSMo 1986; Brophy, 497 N.E. 2d at 634. In this case, only the state's interest in the preservation of life is implicated." Id., at 419.

[8] "The state's concern with the sanctity of life rests on the principle that life is precious and worthy of preservation without regard to its quality." Ibid.
    "It is tempting to equate the state's interest in the preservation of life with some measure of quality of life. As the discussion which follows shows, some courts find quality of life a convenient focus when justifying the termination of treatment. But the state's interest is not in quality of life. The broad policy statements of the legislature make no such distinction; nor shall we. Were quality of life at issue, persons with all manner of handicaps might find the state seeking to terminate their lives. Instead, the state's interest is in life; that interest is unqualified." Id., at 420.
    "As we previously stated, however, the state's interest is not in quality of life. The State's interest is an unqualified interest in life." Id., at 422. "The argument made her, that Nancy will not recover, is but a thinly veiled statement that her life in its present form is not worth living. Yet a diminished quality of life does not support a decision to cause death." Ibid.
    "Given the fact that Nancy is alive and that the burdens of her treatment are not excessive for her, we do not believe her right to

75

refuse treatment, whether that right proceeds from a constitutional right of privacy or a common law right to refuse treatment, outweighs the immense, clear fact of life in which the state maintains a vital interest." Id., at 424.

[9] See especially ante, at 17 ("we think a State may properly decline to make judgments about the 'quality' of life that a particular individual may enjoy, and simply assert an unqualified interest in the preservation of human life to be weighed against the constitutionally protected interests of the individual"); ante, at 18, n. 10 (stating that the government is seeking to protect "its own institutional interests" in life).

[10] See e.g., ante, at 19-20.

[11] "Until the latter part of this century, medicine had relatively little treatment to offer the dying and the vast majority of persons died at home rather than in the hospital." Brief for American Medical Association et. al. as Amici Curiae 6. "In 1985, 83% of deaths [of] Americans age 65 or over occurred in a hospital or nursing home. Sager, Easterling, et. al., Changes in the Location of Death After Passage of Medicare's Prospective Payment System: A National Study, 320 New Eng. J. Med. 433, 435 (1989)." Id., at 6, n. 2.
 According to the President's Commission for the Study of Ethical Problems in Medicine and Biomedical and Behavioral Research:
 "Just as recent years have seen alterations in the underlying causes of death, the places where people die have also changed. For most of recorded history, deaths (of natural causes) usually occurred in the home. "'Everyone knew about death at first hand; there was nothing unfamiliar or even queer about the phenomenon. People seem to have known a lot more about the process itself than is the case today. The "deathbed" was a real place, and the dying person usually knew where he was and when it was time to assemble the family and call for the priest.'
"Even when people did get admitted to a medical care institution, those whose conditions proved incurable were discharged to the care of their families. This was not only because the health care system could no longer be helpful, but also because alcohol and opiates (the only drugs available to ease pain and suffering) were available without a prescription. Institutional care was reserved for the poor or those without family support; hospitals often aimed more at saving patients souls than at providing medical care.
 "As medicine has been able to do more for dying patients, their care has increasingly been delivered in institutional settings. By 1949, institutions were the sites of 50% of all deaths; by 1958, the figure was 61%; and by 1977, over 70%. Perhaps 80% of all deaths in the United States now occur in hospitals and long-term care institutions, such as nursing homes. The change in where very ill patients are treated permits health care professionals to marshall the instruments of scientific medicine more effectively. But people who are dying may well find such a setting alienating and unsupportive," Deciding to Forego Life-Sustaining Treatment 17-18 (1983) (footnotes omitted), quoting, Thomas, Dying as Failure, 447 Annals Am. Acad. Pol. & Sci. 1,3 (1980).

[12] We have recognized that the special relationship between patient and physician will often be encompassed within the domain of private life protected by the Due Process Clause. See, e.g., Griswold v. Connecticut, 381 U.S. 479, 481 (1965); Roe v. Wade, 410 U.S. 113, 152-153 (1973); Thornburgh v. American College of Obstetricians and Gynecologists, 476 U.S. 747, 759 (1986).

[13] The Court recognizes that "the State has been involved as an adversary from the beginning: in this case only because Nancy Cruzan "was a patient at a state hospital when this litigation commenced," ante, at 17, n. 9. It seems to me, however, that the Court draws precisely the wrong conclusion from this insight. The Court apparently believes that the absence of the State from the litigation would have created a problem, because agreement among the family and the independent guardian ad litem as to Nancy Cruzan's best interests might have prevented her treatment from becoming the focus of a "truly adversarial" proceeding. Ibid. It may reasonably be debated whether some judicial process should be required before life-sustaining treatment is discontinued; this issue has divided the state courts. Compare In re Estate of Longeway, 133 Ill. 2d 33, 51, 549 N.E. 2d 292, 300 91989) (requiring judicial approval of guardian's decision) with In re Hamlin, 102 Wash. 2d 810, 818-819, 689 P. 2d 1372, 1377-1378 (1984) (discussing circumstances in which judicial approval is unnecessary). Cf. In re Torres, 357 N.W. 2d 332, 341, n. 4 (Minn. 1984) ("At oral argument it was disclosed that on an average about 10 life support systems are disconnected weekly in Minnesota"). I tend, however, to agree with Judge Blackmar that the intervention of the State in these proceeding as an adversary is not so much a cure as it is part of the disease.

[14] See ante, at 5; ante, at 13. "No right is held more sacred, or is more carefully guarded, by the common law, than the right of every individual to the possession and control of his own person, free from all restraint or interference of others, unless by clear and unquestionable authority of law." Union Pacific R. Co. v. Botsford, 141 U.S. 250, 251 (1891).

[15] Many philosophies and religions have, for example, long venerated the idea that there is a "life after death," and that the human soul endures even after the human body has perished. Surely Missouri would not wish to define its interest in life in a way antithetical to this tradition.

[16] See e.g., H. Johnston, Nathan Hale 1776; Biography and Memorials 128-129 (1914); J. Axelrad, Patrick Henry: The Voice of Freedom 110-111 (1947).

[17] A. Lincoln, Gettysburg Address, 1 Documents of American History (H. Commager ed.) (9th ed. 1973).

[18] The Supreme Judicial Court of Massachusetts observed in this connection: "When we balance the State's interest in prolonging a patient's life against the rights of the patient to reject such prolongation, we must recognize that the state's interest in life encompasses a broader interest than mere corporeal existence. In

certain, thankfully rare, circumstances the burden of maintaining the corporeal existence degrades the very humanity it was meant to serve." Brophy v. New England Sinai Hospital, Inc., 398 Mass. 417, 433-434, 497 N.E. 2d 626, 635 (1986). The Brophy court then stressed that this reflection upon the nature of the State's interest in life was distinguishable from any considerations related to the quality of a particular patient's life, considerations which the court regarded as irrelevant to this inquiry. See also In re Eichner, 73 App. Div. 2d 431, 465, 426 N.Y.S. 2d 517, 543 (1980) (A patient in a persistent vegetative state "has no health, and, in the true sense, no life, for the State to protect"), modified in In re Storar, 52 N.Y. 2d 363, 420 N.E. 2d 64 (1981).

[19] One learned observer suggests, in the course of discussing persistent vegetative states, that "few of us would accept the preservation of such a reduced level of function as a proper goal for medicine, even though we daily accept it as an unfortunate and unforeseen result of treatment that had higher aspirations, and even if we refuse actively to cause such vegetative life to cease." L. Kass, Toward a More Natural Science 203 (1985). This assessment may be controversial. nevertheless, I again tend to agree with Judge Blackmar, who in his dissent from the Missouri Supreme Court's decision contended that it would be unreasonable for the State to assume that most people did in fact hold a view contrary to the one described by Dr. Kass.

My view is further buttressed by the comments of the President's Commission for the Study of Ethical Problems in Medicine and Biomedical and Behavioral Research:
"The primary basis for medical treatment of patients is the prospect that each individual's interests) specifically, the interest in well-being) will be promoted. Thus, treatment ordinarily aims to benefit a patient through preserving life, relieving pain and suffering, protecting against disability, and returning maximally effective functioning. If a prognosis of permanent unconsciousness is correct, however, continued treatment cannot confer such benefits. Pain and suffering are absent, as are joy, satisfaction, and pleasure. Disability is total and no return to an even minimal level of social or human functioning is possible. Deciding to Forego Life-Sustaining Treatment 181-182 (1983).

[20] It is this sense of the word that explains its use to describe a biography: for example, Boswell's Life of Johnson or Beveridge's The Life of John Marshall. The reader of a book so titled would be surprised to find that it contained a compilation of biological data.

[21] See, e.g., In re estate of Longeway, 131, Ill. 2d 33, 549 N.E. 2d 292 (1989) (authorizing removal of a gastronomy tube from a permanently unconscious patient after judicial approval is obtained); McConnell v. Beverly Enterprises - Connecticut, Inc., 209 Conn. 692, 705, 553 A. 2d 596, 603 (1989) (authorizing, pursuant to statute, removal of a gastronomy tube from patient in a persistent vegetative state, where patient had previously expressed a wish not to have treatment sustained); Gray v. Romeo, 697 F. Supp. 580 (RI 1988) (authorizing removal of a feeding tube from a patient in a persistent vegetative state); Rasmussen v. Fleming, 154 Ariz. 207, 741 P. 2d 674 (1987) (en

banc) (authorizing procedures for the removal of a feeding tube from a patient in a persistent vegetative state; In re Gardner, 534 A. 2d 947 (Me. 1987) (allowing discontinuation of life-sustaining procedures for a patient in a persistent vegetative state); In re Peter, 108 N.J. 365, 529 A. 2d 419 (1987) (authorizing procedures for cessation of treatment to elderly nursing home patient in a persistent vegetative state); In re Jobes, 108 N.J. 394, 529 A. 2d 434 (1987) (authorizing procedures for cessation of treatment to nonelderly patient determined by "clear and convincing" evidence to be a persistent vegetative state); Brophy v. New England Sinai Hospital, Inc., 398 Mass. 417, 497 N.E. 2d 626 (1986) (permitting removal of a feeding tube from a patient in a persistent vegetative state); John F. Kennedy Memorial Hospital, Inc. v. Bludworth, 451 So. 2d 921 (Fla. 1984) (holding that court approval was not needed to authorize cessation of life-support fro patient in a persistent vegetative state who had executed a living will); In re Torres, 357 N.W. 2d 332 (Minn. 1984) (authorizing removal of a permanently unconscious patient from life-support systems); In re L.H.R., 253 Ga. 439, 321 S.E. 2d 716 (1984) (allowing parents to terminate life support for infant in a chronic vegetative state); In re Hamlin, 102 wash. 2d 810, 689 P. 2d 1372 (1984) (allowing termination, without judicial intervention, of life support for patient in a vegetative state if doctors and guardian concur; conflicts among doctors and the guardian with respect to cessation of treatment are to be resolved by a trial court); In re Colyer, 99 Wash. 2d 114, 660 P. 2d 738 (1983), modified on other grounds, In re Hamlin, 102 Wash. 2d 810, 689 P. 2d 1372 (1984) (allowing court-appointed guardian to authorize cessation of treatment of patient in persistent vegetative state); In re Eichner (decided with In re Storar), 52 N.Y. 2d 363, 420 N.E. 2d 64, cert. denied, 454 U.S. 858 (1981) (authorizing the removal of a patient in a persistent vegetative state from a respirator); In re Quinlan, 70 N.J. 10, 355 A. 2d 647, cert. denied, 429 U.S. 922 91976) (authorizing, on constitutional grounds, the removal of a patient in a persistent vegetative state from a respirator); Corbett v. D'Alessandro, 487 So. 2d 368 (Fla. App. 1986) (authorizing removal of nasogastric feeding tube from patient in persistent vegetative state); In re Drabick, 200 Cal. App. 3d 185, 218, 245, Cal. Rptr. 840, 861 (1988) ("Life sustaining treatment is not 'necessary' under Probate Code section 2355 if it offers no reasonable possibility of returning the conservatee to cognitive life and if it is not otherwise in the conservatee's best interest, as determined by the conservator in good faith"). Delio v. Westchester County Medical Center, 129 App. Div. 2d 1, 516 N.Y.S. 2d 677 (1987) (authorizing discontinuation of artificial feeding for a 33-year-old patient in a persistent vegetative state); Leach v. Akron General Medical Center, 68 Ohio Misc. 1, 426 N.E. 2d 809 (1980) (authorizing removal of a patient in a persistent vegetative state from a respirator); In re Severns 425 A. 2d 156 (Del. Ch. 1980) (authorizing discontinuation of all medical support measures for a patient in a "virtual vegetative state").

These cases are not the only ones which have allowed the cessation of life-sustaining treatment to incompetent patients. See e.g., Superintendant of Belchertown State School v. Saikewicz, 373 Mass. 728, 370 N.E. 2d. 417 (1977) (holding that treatment could have been withheld from a profoundly mentally retarded patient); Bouvia v. Superior Court of Los Angeles, 225 Cal. Rptr. 297 (1986) (Allowing removal of life-saving nasogastric tube from competent, highly intelligent patient who was in extreme pain).

22 Although my reasoning entails the conclusion that the best interests of the incompetent patient must be respected even when the patient is conscious, rather than in a vegetative state, considerations pertaining to the a"quality of life," in addition to considerations about the definition of life, might then be relevant. The State's interest in protecting the life, and thereby the interests, of the incompetent patient would accordingly be more forceful, and the constitutional questions would be correspondingly complicated.

23 Thus, the state court wrote:
"This State has expressed a strong policy favoring life. We believe that policy dictates that we err on the side of preserving life. If there is to be a change in that policy, it must come from the people through their elected representatives. Broad policy questions bearing on life and death issued are more properly addressed by representative assemblies. These have vast fact and opinion gathering and synthesizing powers unavailable to courts; the exercise of these powers is particularly appropriate where issues invoke the concerns of medicine, ethics, morality, philosophy, theology and law. Assuming change is appropriate, this issue demands a comprehensive resolution which courts cannot provide." 760 S.W. 2d, at 426.

24 The Supreme Judicial Court of Massachusetts anticipated this possibility in its Brophy decision, where it observed that the "duty of the State to preserve life must encompass a recognition of an individual's right to avoid circumstances in which the individual himself would feel that efforts to sustain life demean or degrade his humanity," because otherwise the State's defense of life would be tantamount to an effort by "the State to make decisions regarding the individual's quality of life." 398 Mass., at 434, 497 N.E. 2d, at 635. Accord, Gray v. Romeo, 697 F. Supp., at 588.

25 Judge Campbell said on behalf of the Florida District Court of Appeal for the Second District:
"We want to acknowledge that we began our deliberations in this matter, as did those who drafted our Declaration of Independence, with the solemnity and the gratefulness of the knowledge 'that all men are ... endowed by their Creator with ... Life." It was not without considerable searching of our hearts, souls, and minds, as well as the jurisprudence of this great Land that we have reached our conclusions. We forcefully affirm that Life having been endowed by our Creator should not be lightly taken nor relinquished. We recognize, however, that we are also endowed with a certain amount of dignity and the right to the 'Pursuit of Happiness.' when, therefore, it may be determined by reason of the advanced scientific and medical technologies of this day that Life has, through cause beyond our control, reached the unconscious and vegetative state where all that remains is the forced function of the body's vital functions, including the artificial sustenance of the body itself, then we recognize the right to allow the natural consequence of the removal of those artificial life sustaining measures" Corbett v. D'Alessandro, 487 So. 2d, at 371.

NATURAL DEATH WITH DIGNITY:

PROTECTING YOUR RIGHT TO REFUSE MEDICAL TREATMENT

CHAPTER 4 —

STATUTORY LIVING WILLS

Now that you have read our own personal story and the <u>Cruzan</u> case, you should be convinced to take the necessary steps to protect yourself and your family from the possibility of similar occurrences.

Under present law in this country, we have identified three basic steps we believe need to be completed. First, you must prepare a living will in conformity with the law of your state. Second, prepare a personalized detailed statement of intent regarding the withholding or limiting of medical consent. Third, provide a durable power of attorney to a third person who can exercise decisions regarding medical consent, in those circumstances where you are incapable of giving or refusing consent yourself.

All three steps may or may not be able to be accomplished in one document. Each and every state has different laws addressing these issues and the laws of the particular state you reside in must be complied with to protect the enforceability of your intent. It is not the intent of this book to provide you with specific legal advice on your particular circumstances or for you to circumvent consulting with an attorney. To properly draft and execute the necessary documentation will require you to consult with an attorney before you complete the entire process. However, this book should serve as a basic guide to inform you as to the general issues that must be addressed and provide you with an outline to take to your attorney before drafting any final documents. Further, it is recommended you take this book with you when you consult with your attorney, as this is an evolving area of the law and a particular attorney may not have researched or be well versed in this subject matter. This book would help your attorney become familiar with the issues, and the resources and reference information contained in the back of the book would be an invaluable resource to both you and your attorney.

Do not be afraid to contact an attorney or consult with an attorney. There are simply sometimes in our complex modern society that professional advice and consultation is necessary. Just as it is sometimes necessary to see a doctor for health care, or for an accountant to prepare your taxes, it is sometimes necessary to consult with an attorney.

This is not to say you should not be an informed consumer of legal services and prepare for that consultation. This book will help you do that. Being familiar with the following recommended steps, and having a clear idea of what you want to accomplish, should substantially reduce the amount of attorney's time needed to assist you, and thus reduce any legal fees. If you are concerned about attorney fees or costs in preparing these necessary documents, you should consult with the attorney you select regarding his fees. Explain to the attorney you are familiar with the subject matter and have prepared some documents for him to review. If you consult with an attorney who you have an established relationship with, or have consulted with on other matters, the attorney might well agree to review the documents for you at no charge or a nominal charge. If the attorney you consult with advises you he would not be able to review your documents without a substantial retainer or estimate to you a substantial fee, you might consider consulting with another attorney.   In any case, whatever it may cost you to have these documents reviewed, may well be the best money you ever spend in your life, considering the peace of mind it may give you and the potential future security it will provide.

The first step then is the statutory living will. A living will is an advanced directive to guide health care providers regarding health care decisions for you at the end of your life. At this point, the most important thing to remember is the statutory living will statutes generally do not apply to all situations. However, it is a good place to begin our process and inquiry.

Begin by looking up the form applicable to your State under your own state heading. Each state that provided a form in its statutes have been reproduced in the following pages. At the top of the page, a reference is made to the particular state statute so you or your attorney may review the entire act passed in your state. It is important to review the source legislation for several reasons. Primarily, it is important to understand the statutory definitions of terms used within the declaration. You will note as you read through your state's form there are many possible circumstances that will not be addressed by the basic outline provided within these statutes. You must review the form with your attorney, looking to the statutory definitions, to see to it whether the form sufficiently covers your circumstances, and whether any deviation from the form is allowed or recommended.

If at sometime in the past someone has simply provided to you a blank general form and requested you to fill it out, and you did so, we suggest to you to re-think that previous act and review that document at this time. The first form provided in the following pages is drafted from the Uniform Rights of the Terminally Ill Act. This was a proposed model act provided to the various states for their consideration in drafting legislation. This model form was simply a proposal to the states and is not law itself. However, many groups, organizations, and individuals have circulated substantially this form and encourage people to complete the form. We are providing this cautionary advice regarding the model act form because as you can see from the following pages, most state legislatures have substantially modified the proposed act form, and some states have mandated their form be followed in substantially the same form as provided by their state statutes.

When this book went to press, 43 states and the District of Columbia had passed some legislation touching upon living wills or health care proxies. Nebraska, New Jersey, Pennsylvania, and Rhode Island did not have laws on the books at the time of publishing, but did have bills pending. Consult with your local library, state law library, or your attorney to see if laws have been passed in these states subsequent to the date of publishing of this book. Statutory forms for Massachusetts and Michigan were not available at press time. When we went to press, Ohio, South Dakota, and Kentucky were the only states known not to have any legislation on the books or pending. If you live in one of these states, it would be a good idea to contact your local legislator and encourage him or her to sponsor or support living will legislation.

It is recommended you fill out, sign and have properly witnessed one of these state forms if you agree with all of its limitations. At the very least, you would have protection for the limited circumstances the declaration provides for. However, if you want to go beyond the form, or you disagree or do not fully understand the meaning or implication of any of the restrictions, conditions, or language of the official form, then it is recommended you consult with an attorney regarding the issues raised by the language in the state form you question, or the additional language you may like to add but is not contained within the state form. If you reside in a state that has not yet passed legislation, use as a starting worksheet the first form provided, that being the Uniform Rights of the Terminally Ill Act model form. Use this only as a drafting guide and consult with a local attorney regarding the implications of executing a living will in a state which does not statutorily authorize living wills.

Dealing with restrictions or issues raised by the various state forms is addressed more fully in the next chapter.

Many living will statutes have been sharply criticized for the ambiguity created by their language, and the broad discretion often granted the health care provider in interpreting that language. The meaning and specific intent of certain words employed by the various declarations may be insufficiently clear to provide you, when you execute such a general declaration, notice of what would be the effect of the declaration. The ambiguity created by some of the language has been criticized as granting to physicians excessively broad discretionary authority to determine when a living will would become effective.

Some of the following terms or phrases can be criticized for creating ambiguity. What does "relatively short time" mean? Does it mean death must be imminent or may it occur within a year or two over the course of a final illness. What does "terminal condition" mean? Is this a condition that will bring about death in a matter of days or weeks, or is it a condition that can drag on for years before a person's death. What does "life sustaining treatment" mean or "comfort care" mean? Would this mean only medications or would it include nutrition or hydration? Almost all declarations require the person have an incurable or irreversible condition that will cause the person's death within a relatively short period of time. But what if you are in a persistent vegetative state or comatose, and death is not imminent or even likely to occur in a relatively short period of time? As you have seen in the proceeding chapters, you could very easily live thirty years in a comatose condition or persistent vegetative state with the administration of tube feedings and hydration. If you want to address or resolve these issues, then modification, deviation, or expansion of the state statutory form may be necessary.

If this is the case, use your state form as a drafting guide to address these issues with your own conscience, considering your own morals and religious beliefs. Once you have done that, you are ready to proceed to the next chapter. If you are satisfied with the state form, understand the definitions and the various terms contained within the form, and understand the general statutory intent and impact of the form, then we still suggest you contact an attorney to determine if the form is currently valid in your state. If you insist on executing one of the forms without consulting an attorney, we highly recommend and advise you to read your entire state act dealing with living wills, and any state case law decided interpreting the act. If you sign one of these forms, also make certain the form was properly executed. Never have a relative or any person who might be interested in your estate witness the signature on the living will. Many state statutes require this safeguard, and in any case, it is a good idea.

Lastly, a living will has no value at all if it is not properly communicated and made available to those who need to know. Make multiple copies of any completed living will and make it available to your health care provider. Discuss your wishes with your family physician if you have one, and request it be made a part of your medical records. Discuss your wishes and desires with members of your family and keep copies of your living will with your personal papers readily available so a member of your family or a close friend could access them easily with short notice. A living will locked inside a safety deposit box will do you little good under these circumstances. You might even consider using some modern photo copying equipment that has the ability to reduce, and reduce your living will to a size easily carried in your wallet or purse. A copy of your living will should also be filed with your attorney and any minister you may have.

DECLARATION FROM

UNIFORM RIGHTS OF THE TERMINALLY ILL ACT

A PROPOSED MODEL ACT

Section 2

A declaration may, but need not, be in the following form:

DECLARATION

If I should have an incurable or irreversible condition that will cause my death within a relatively short time, and I am no longer able to make decisions regarding my medical treatment, direct my attending physician, pursuant to the Uniform Rights of the Terminally Ill Act of this State, to withhold or withdraw treatment that only prolongs the process of dying and is not necessary to my comfort or to alleviate pain.

Signed this _____ day of _____, 19___.

Signed _____
Address _____

The declarant voluntarily signed this writing in my presence.

Witness _____
Address _____
Witness _____
Address _____

DISTRICT OF COLUMBIA

NATURAL DEATH

Section 6-2422

The declaration shall be substantially in the following form:

DECLARATION

Declaration made this _____ day of _____, 19_____.
I, _____ being of sound mind, willfully and voluntarily make known my desires that my dying shall not be artificially prolonged under the circumstances set forth below, do declare:
If at any time I should have an incurable injury, disease, or illness certified to be a terminal condition by 2 physicians who have personally examined me, one of whom shall be my attending physician, and the physicians have determined that my death will occur whether or not life-sustaining procedures are utilized and where the application of life-sustaining procedures would serve only at artificially prolong the dying process, I direct that such procedures be withheld or withdrawn, and that I be permitted to die naturally with only the administration of medication or the performance of any medical procedures deemed necessary to provide me with comfort care or to alleviate pain.
In the absence of my ability to give directions regarding the use of such life-sustaining procedures, it is my intention that this declaration shall be honored by my family and physician(s) as the final expression of my legal right to refuse medical or surgical treatment and accept the consequences from such refusal.
I understand the full import of this declaration and I am emotionally and mentally competent to make this declaration.

Signed _____
Address _____

I believe the declarant to be of sound mind. I did not sign the declarant's signature above for or at the direction of the declarant. I am at least 18 years of age and am not related to the declarant by blood or marriage, entitled to any portion of the estate of the declarant according to the laws of intestate succession of the District of Columbia or under any will of the declarant or codicil thereto, or directly financially responsible for declarant's medical care. I am not the declarant's attending physician, an employee of the attending physician, or an employee of the health facility in which the declarant is a patient.

Witness _____
Witness _____

TERMINATION OF LIFE-SUPPORT PROCEDURES

Section 22-8A-5

The declaration shall be substantially in the following form, but in addition may include other specific directions. SHould any of the other specific directions be held to be invalid, such invalidity shall not affect other directions of the declaration which can be given effect without the invalid direction, and to this end the directions in the declaration are severable.

DECLARATION

Declaration made this _____ day of _____, 19___. I, _____, being of sound mind, willfully and voluntarily make known my desires that my dying shall not be artificially prolonged under the circumstances set forth below, do hereby declare:

If at any time I should have an incurable injury, disease, or illness certified to be a terminal condition by two physicians who have personally examined me, one of whom shall be my attending physician, and the physicians have determined that my death will occur whether or not life-sustaining procedures would serve only to artificially prolong the dying process, I direct that such procedures be withheld or withdrawn, and that I be permitted to die naturally with only the administration of medication or the performance of any medical procedure deemed necessary to provide me with comfort care.

I the absence of my ability to give directions regarding the use of such life-sustaining procedures, it is my intention that this declaration shall be honored by my family and physician(s) as the final expression of my legal right to refuse medical or surgical treatment and accept the consequences from such refusal.

I understand the full import of this declaration and I am emotionally and mentally competent to make this declaration.

Signed _____

City, County and State of Residence _____

_____

_____

Date _____

The declarant has been personally known to me and I believe him or her to be of sound mind. I did not sign the declarant's signature above for or at the direction of the declarant. I am not related to the declarant by blood or marriage, entitled to any portion of the estate of the declarant according to the laws of intestate succession or under any will of declarant or codicil thereto, or directly financially responsible for declarant's medical care.

Witness _____
Witness _____

Date _____

ALASKA

RIGHTS OF TERMINALLY ILL

Section 18.12.010

A declaration may, but need not, be in the following form:

DECLARATION

If I should have an incurable or irreversible condition that will cause my death within a relatively short time, it is my desire that my life not be prolonged by administration of life-sustaining procedures.

If my condition is terminal and I am unable to participate in decisions regarding my medical treatment, I direct my attending physician to withhold or withdraw procedures that merely prolong the dying process and are not necessary to my comfort or to alleviate pain.

I [ ] do [ ] do not desire that nutrition or hydration (food and water) be provided by gastric tube or intravenously if necessary.

Signed this _____ day of _____, 19___.

Signature _____
Place _____

The declarant is known to me and voluntarily signed or voluntarily directed another to sign this document in my presence.

Witness _____
Address _____
Witness _____
Address _____

State of _____, _____ Judicial District

The foregoing instrument was acknowledged before me this _____ day of _____, 19___, by _____.

_____

Signature of Person Taking Acknowledgment

_____

Title or Rank

_____

Serial Number, if any

THIS DECLARATION MUST BE EITHER WITNESSED BY TWO PERSON OR ACKNOWLEDGED BY A PERSON QUALIFIED TO TAKE ACKNOWLEDGMENTS UNDER AS 09.63.010.

ARIZONA

MEDICAL TREATMENT DECISION ACT

Section 36-3202

The declaration shall be substantially in the following form but may include other specific directions.

DECLARATION

Declaration made this _____ day of _____, 19___. I, _____, being of sound mind, willfully and voluntarily make known my desire that my dying not be artificially prolonged under the circumstances set forth below and declare that:

If at any time I should have an incurable injury, disease or illness certified to be a terminal condition by two physicians who have personally examined me, one of whom is my attending physician, and the physicians have determined that my death will occur unless life-sustaining procedures are used and if the application of life-sustaining procedures would serve only to artificially prolong the dying process, I direct that life-sustaining procedures be withheld or withdrawn and that I be permitted to die naturally with only the administration of medication, food or fluids or the performance of medical procedures deemed necessary to provide me with comfort care.

In the absence of my ability to give directions regarding the use of life-sustaining procedures, it is my intention that this declaration be honored by my family and attending physician as the final expression of my legal right to refuse medical or surgical treatment and accept the consequences from such refusal.

I understand the full import of this declaration and I have emotional and mental capacity to make this declaration.

Signed _____

City, County and State of residence _____

The declarant is personally known to me and I believe him / her to be of sound mind.

Witness _____
Witness _____

ARKANSAS

ARKANSAS RIGHTS OF THE TERMINALLY ILL OR PERMANENTLY UNCONSCIOUS ACT

Section 20-17-202

A declaration may, but need not, be in the following form in the case where the patient has a terminal condition.

DECLARATION

If I should have an incurable or irreversible condition that will cause my death within a relatively short time or if I should become permanently unconscious, and I am no longer able to make decisions regarding my medical treatment, I direct my attending physician, pursuant to the Arkansas Rights of the Terminally Ill or Permanently Unconscious Act, to [withhold or withdraw treatment that only prolongs the process of dying and is not necessary to my comfort or to alleviate pain] [follow the instructions of _____ whom I appoint as my Health care Proxy to decide whether life-sustaining treatment should be withheld or withdrawn].

Signed this _____ day of _____, 19___.

Signature _____
Address _____

The declarant voluntarily signed this writing in my presence.

Witness _____
Address _____
Witness _____
Address _____

CALIFORNIA

NATURAL DEATH ACT

Section 7188

The directive shall be in the following form:

DIRECTIVE TO PHYSICIANS

Directive made this _____ day of _____, 19___.

I, _____, being of sound mind, willfully, and voluntarily make known my desire that my life shall not be artificially prolonged under the circumstances set forth below, do hereby declare:

1. If at any time I should have an incurable injury, disease, or illness certified to be a terminal condition by two physicians, and where the application of life-sustaining procedures would serve only to artificially prolong the moment of my death and where my physician determines that my death is imminent whether or not life-sustaining procedures are utilized, I direct that such procedures be withheld or withdrawn, and that I be permitted to die naturally.

2. In the absence of my ability to give directions regarding the use of such life-sustaining procedures, it is my intention that this directive shall be honored by my family and physician(s) as the final expression of my legal right to refuse medical or surgical treatment and accept the consequences from such refusal.

3. If I have been diagnosed as pregnant and that diagnosis is known to my physician, this directive shall have no force or effect during the course of my pregnancy.

4. I have been diagnosed and notified at least 14 days ago as having a terminal condition by _____, M.D., whose address is _____, and whose telephone number is _____. I understand that if I have not filled in the physician's name and address, it shall be presumed that I did not have a terminal condition when I made out this directive.

5. This directive shall have no force or effect five years from the date filled in above.

6. I understand the full import of this directive and I am emotionally and mentally competent to make this directive.

Signed _____

City, County and State of Residence _____

The declarant has been personally known to me and I believe him or her to be of sound mind.

Witness _____
Witness _____

COLORADO MEDICAL TREATMENT DECISION ACT

Section 15-18-104

The declaration may, but need not be, in the following form:

DECLARATION AS TO MEDICAL OR SURGICAL TREATMENT

I, _____, being of sound mind and at least eighteen years of age, direct that my life shall not be artificially prolonged under the circumstances set forth below and hereby declare that:

1. If at any time my attending physician and one other physician certify in writing that:

a. I have an injury, disease, or illness which is not curable or reversible and which, in their judgment, is a terminal condition; and

b. For a period of forty-eight consecutive hours or more, I have been unconscious, comatose, or otherwise incompetent so as to be unable to make or communicate responsible decisions concerning my person; then

I direct that life-sustaining procedures shall be withdrawn and withheld, it being understood that life-sustaining procedures shall not include any medical procedure or intervention for nourishment or considered necessary by the attending physician to provide comfort or alleviate pain.

2. I execute this declaration, as my free and voluntary act, this _____ day of _____, 19____.

By _____

The foregoing instrument was signed and declared by _____ to be his declaration, in the presence of us, who, in his presence, in the presence of each other, and at his request, have signed our names below as witnesses, and we declare that, at the time of the execution of this instrument, the declarant, according to our best knowledge and belief, was of sound mind and under no constraint or undue influence.

DATED at _____, Colorado, this _____ day of _____, 19____.

_____
Name and address

_____
Name and address

STATE OF COLORADO   )
                    : ss.
County of _____)

     SUBSCRIBED and sworn to before me by _____, the declarant, and _____, and _____), witnesses, as the voluntary act and deed of the declarant, this _____ day of _____, 19___.

     My commission expires:

                          _____
                          Notary Public

CONNECTICUT

REMOVAL OF LIFE SUPPORT SYSTEMS

Section 19a-575

Any adult person may execute a document in substantially the following form:

REMOVAL OF LIFE SUPPORT SYSTEMS

If the time comes when I am incapacitated to the point when I can no longer actively take part in decisions for my own life, and am unable to direct my physician as to my own medical care, I wish this statement to stand as a testament of my wishes. I, _____, request that I be allowed to die and not be kept alive through life support systems if my condition is deemed terminal. I do not intend any direct taking of my life, but only that my dying not be unreasonably prolonged. This request is made, after careful reflection, while I am of sound mind.

DATED this _____ day of _____, 19___.

_____

Witness _____
Witness _____

DELAWARE

PATIENT'S RIGHT TO TERMINATE TREATMENT

Section 2503

No form is provided by statute. However, the following instructions are provided by statute:

EXECUTION OF DECLARATION

(a) Any adult person may execute a declaration directing the withholding or withdrawal of maintenance medical treatment, where the person is in a terminal condition and under such circumstances as may be set forth in the declaration. The declaration made pursuant to this chapter shall be:

(1) In writing;
(2) Signed by the person making the declaration, or by another person in the declarant's presence and at the declarant's expressed direction;
(3) Dated; and
(4) Signed in the presence of 2 or more adult witnesses, as set forth in subsection (b) of this section.

(b) The declaration shall be signed by the declarant in the presence of 2 subscribing witnesses, neither of whom:

(1) Is related to the declarant by blood or marriage;
(2) Is entitled to any portion of the estate of the declarant under any will of the declarant or codicil thereto then existing nor, at the time of the declaration, is entitled by operation of law then existing;
(3) Has, at the time of the execution of the declaration, a present or inchoate claim against any portion of the estate of the declarant;
(4) Has a direct financial responsibility for the declarant's medical care; or
(5) Is an employee of the hospital or other health care facility in which the declarant is a patient.

(c) Each witness to the declaration shall state in writing that he is not prohibited under subsection (b) of this section from being a witness under this chapter.

(d) The declaration of a patient diagnosed as pregnant by the attending physician shall be of no effect during the course of the patient's pregnancy. Where a declaration is lacking any requirement under this section and such defect is later corrected by amendment or codicil, whether formally or informally prepared, such declaration shall be valid ab initio, notwithstanding the earlier defect.

FLORIDA

LIFE-PROLONGING PROCEDURE ACT OF FLORIDA

Section 765.05

A declaration executed pursuant to Section 765.04 may, but need not, be in the following form:

DECLARATION

Declaration made this _____ day of _____, 19___. I, _____, willfully and voluntarily make known my desire that my dying not be artificially prolonged under the circumstances set forth below, and I do hereby declare:

If at any time I should have a terminal condition and if my attending physician has determined that there can be no recovery from such condition and that my death is imminent, I direct that life-prolonging procedures be withheld or withdrawn when the application of such procedures would serve only to prolong artificially the process of dying, and that I be permitted to die naturally with only the administration of medication or the performance of any medical procedure deemed necessary to provide me with comfort care or to alleviate pain.

In the absence of my ability to give directions regarding the use of such life-prolonging procedures, it is my intention that this declaration be honored by my family and physician as the final expression of my legal right to refuse medical or surgical treatment and to accept the consequences for such refusal.

If I have been diagnosed as pregnant and that diagnosis is known to my physician, this declaration shall have no force or effect during the course of my pregnancy.

I understand the full import of this declaration, and I am emotionally and mentally competent to make this declaration.

_____
(Signed)

The declarant is know to me, and I believe him or her to be of sound mind.

_____
Witness

_____
Witness

LIVING WILLS

Section 88-4103

The form for the declaration shall be substantially as follows:

LIVING WILL

Living will made this _____ day of _____, 19___.
I, _____, being of sound mind, willfully and voluntarily make known my desire that my life shall not be prolonged under the circumstances set forth below and do declare:

1. If at any time I should have a terminal condition as defined in and established in accordance with the procedures set forth in paragraph (10) of Code Section 31-32-2 of the Official Code of Georgia Annotated, I direct that the application of life-sustaining procedures to my body be withheld or withdrawn and that I be permitted to die;

2. In the absence of my ability to give directions regarding the use of such life-sustaining procedures, it is my intention that this living will shall be honored by my family and physician(s) as the final expression of my legal right to refuse medical or surgical treatment and accept the consequences from such refusal;

3. I understand that I may revoke this living will at any time;

4. I understand the full import of this living will, and I am at least 18 years of age and am emotionally and mentally competent to make this living will; and

5. If I am female and I have been diagnosed as pregnant, this living will shall have no force and effect during the course of my pregnancy.

Signed _____

_____ (City) _____ (County) _____ (State)

I hereby witness this living will and attest that:

(1) The declarant is personally known to me and I believe the declarant to be at least 18 years of age and of sound mind;

(2) I am at least 18 years of age;

(3) To the best of my knowledge, at the time of the execution of this living will, I:

(A) Am not related to the declarant by blood or marriage;

(B) Would not be entitled to any portion of the declarant's estate by any will or by operation of law under the rules of descent and distribution of this state;

    (C) Am not the attending physician of declarant or an employee of the attending physician or an employee of the hospital or skilled nursing facility in which declarant is a patient;

    (D) Am not directly financially responsible for the declarant's medical care; and

    (E) Have no present claim against any portion of the estate of the declarant;

    (4) Declarant has signed this document in my presence as above-instructed, on the date above first shown.

Witness   _____
Address   _____
Witness   _____
Address   _____

    Additional witness required when living will is signed in a hospital or skilled nursing facility.

    I hereby witness this living will and attest that I believe the declarant to be of sound mind and to have this living will willingly and voluntarily.

Witness   _____
Medical director of skilled nursing
facility or staff physician not
participating in care of the patient or
chief of the hospital medical staff or
staff physician not participating in care
of the patient."

HAWAII

MEDICAL TREATMENT DECISIONS

Section 327D-4

A declaration executed pursuant to this chapter requesting that medical treatment be withheld or withdrawn may, but need not, be substantially in the following form, and may include other specific directions.

DECLARATION

A. State of Declarant

Declaration made this _____ day of _____, 19___.
I, _____, being of sound mind, wilfully and voluntarily make known my desire that my dying shall not be artificially prolonged under the circumstances set forth below, and do hereby declare:

If at any time I should have an incurable or irreversible condition certified to be terminal by two physicians who have personally examined me, one of whom shall be my attending physician, and the physicians have determined that I am unable to make decisions concerning my medical treatment, and that without administration of life-sustaining treatment my death will occur in a relatively short time, and where the application of life-sustaining procedures would serve only to prolong artificially the dying process, I direct that such procedures be withheld or withdrawn, and that I be permitted to die naturally with only the administration of medication, nourishment, or fluids or the performance of any medical procedure deemed necessary to provide me with comfort or to alleviate pain.

In the absence of my ability to give directions regarding the use of such life-sustaining procedures, it is my intention that this declaration shall be honored by my family and physician(s) as the final expressions of my legal right to refuse medical or surgical treatment and accept the consequences from such refusal.

I understand the full import of this declaration and I am emotionally and mentally competent to make this declaration.

Signed _____

Address _____

B. Statement of Witnesses

I am at least 18 years of age and
- not related to the declarant by blood, marriage, or adoption; and

101

- not the attending physician, an employee of the attending physician, or an employee of the medical care facility in which the declarant is a patient.

The declarant is personally known to me and I believe the declarant to be of sound mind.

Witness   _____
Address   _____

Witness   _____
Address   _____

C. Notarization

Subscribed, sworn to and acknowledged before me by _____, the declarant, and subscribed and sworn to before me by _____, and _____, witnesses, this ____ day of _____, 19____.

(SEAL)   Signed _____

                                    _____
                                    (Official capacity of officer)

IDAHO

NATURAL DEATH ACT

Section 39-4504

Such document shall be in the following form or in another form that contains the elements set forth in this section.

A LIVING WILL

A Directive to Withhold or to Provide Treatment

To my family, my relative, my friends, my physicians, my employers, and all others whom it may concern:

Directive made this _____ day of _____, 19___.

I, _____, being of sound mind, willfully, and voluntarily make known my desire that my life shall not be prolonged artificially under the circumstances set forth below, do hereby declare:

1. It at any time I should have an incurable injury, disease, illness or condition certified to be terminal by two medical doctors who have examined me, and where the application of life-sustaining procedures of any kind would serve only to prolong artificially the moment of my death, and where a medical doctor determines that my death is imminent, whether or not life-sustaining procedures are utilized, or I have been diagnosed as being in a persistent vegetative state, I direct that the following marked expression of my intent be followed and that I be permitted to die naturally, and that I receive any medical treatment or care that may be required to keep me free of pain or distress.

"Check One Box"

____ If at any time I should become unable to communicate my instruction, then I direct that all medical treatment, care, and nutrition and hydration necessary to restore my health, sustain my life, and to abolish or alleviate pain or distress be provided to me. Nutrition and hydration shall not be withheld or withdrawn from me if I would die from malnutrition or dehydration rather than from my injury, disease, illness or condition.

____ If at any time I should become unable to communicate my instructions and where the application of artificial life-sustaining procedures shall serve only to prolong artificially the moment of my death, I direct such procedures be withheld or withdrawn except for the administration of nutrition and hydration.

____ If at any time I should become unable to communicate my instructions and where the application of artificial life-sustaining procedures shall serve only to prolong artificially the moment of death, I direct such procedures be withheld or withdrawn including withdrawal of the administration of nutrition and hydration.

2. In the absence of my ability to give directions regarding the use of life-sustaining procedures, I hereby appoint _____ currently residing at _____, as my attorney-in-fact proxy for the making of decisions relating to my health care in my place; and it is my intention that this appointment shall be honored by him / her, by my family, relatives, friends, physicians, and lawyer as the final expression of my legal right to refuse medical or surgical treatment; and I accept the consequences of such a decision. I have duly executed a Durable Power of Attorney for health care decisions on this date.

3. In the absence of my ability to give further directions regarding my treatment, including life-sustaining procedures, it is my intention that this directive shall be honored by my family and physicians as the final expression of my legal right to refuse or accept medical and surgical treatment, and I accept the consequences of such refusal.

4. If I have been diagnosed as pregnant and that diagnosis is known to any interested person, this directive shall have no force during the course of my pregnancy.

5. I understand the full importance of this directive and am emotionally and mentally competent to make this directive. No participant in the making of this directive or in its being carried into effect, whether it be a medical doctor, my spouse, a relative, friend or any other person shall be held responsible in any way, legally, professionally or socially, for complying with my directions.

Signed _____

City, County and State of residence _____

The declarant has been known to me personally and I believe him / her to be of sound mind.

Witness _____

Address _____

Witness _____

Address _____

ILLINOIS

LIVING WILL ACT

Section 703-3

The declaration may, but need not, be in the following form, and in addition may include other specific directions.

DECLARATION

This declaration is made this _____ day of _____, 19___. I, _____, being of sound mind, willfully and voluntarily make known my desires that my moment of death shall not be artificially postponed.

If at any time I should have an incurable and irreversible injury, disease, or illness judged to be a terminal condition by my attending physician who has personally examined me and has determined that my death is imminent except for death delaying procedures, I direct that such procedures which would only prolong the dying process be withheld or withdrawn, and that I be permitted to die naturally with only the administration of medication, sustenance, or the performance of any medical procedure deemed necessary by my attending physician to provide me with comfort care.

In the absence of my ability to give directions regarding the use of such death delaying procedures, it is my intention that this declaration shall be honored by my family and physician as the final expression of my legal right to refuse medical or surgical treatment and accept the consequences from such refusal.

Signed _____

City, County, and State of Residence _____

The declarant is personally known to me and I believe him or her to be of sound mind. I saw the declarant sign the declaration in my presence (or the declarant acknowledged in my presence that he or she had signed the declaration) and I signed the declaration as a witness in the presence of the declarant. I did not sign the declarant's signature above for or at the direction of the declarant. At the date of this instrument, I am not entitled to any portion of the estate of the declarant according to the laws of intestate succession or , to the best of my knowledge and belief, under any will of declarant of other instrument taking effect at declarant's death, or directly financially responsible for declarant's medical care.

Witness _____

Witness _____

105

LIVING WILLS AND LIFE-PROLONGING PROCEDURES ACT

Section 16-8-11-12

A declaration must be substantially in the form set forth, but the declaration may include additional, specific directions.

LIVING WILL DECLARATION

Declaration made this _____ day of _____, 19___. I, _____, being at least eighteen (18) years old and of sound mind, willfully and voluntarily make known my desires that my dying shall not be artificially prolonged under the circumstances set forth below, and I declare:

If at any time I have an incurable injury, disease, or illness certified in writing to be a terminal condition by my attending physician, and my attending physician has determined that my death will occur within a short period of time, and the use of life-prolonging procedures would serve only to artificially prolong the dying process, I direct that such procedures be withheld or withdrawn, and that I be permitted to die naturally with only the provision of appropriate nutrition and hydration and the administration of medication and the performance of any medical procedure necessary to provide me with comfort care or to alleviate pain.

In the absence of my ability to give directions regarding the use of life-prolonging procedures, it is my intention that this declaration be honored by my family and physician as the final expression of my legal right to refuse medical or surgical treatment and accept the consequences of the refusal.

I understand the full import of this declaration.

Signed _____

City, County, and State of Residence _____

The declarant has been personally known to me, and I believe (him/her) to be of sound mind. I did not sign the declarant's signature above for or at the direction of the declarant. I am not a parent, spouse, or child of the declarant. I am not entitled to any part of the declarant's estate or directly financially responsible for the declarant's medical care. I am competent and at least eighteen (18) years old.

Witness _____   Date _____

Witness _____   Date _____

106

IOWA

LIFE-SUSTAINING PROCEDURES ACT

Section 144A.3

A declaration executed pursuant to this chapter may, but need not, be in the following form:

DECLARATION

If I should have an incurable or irreversible condition that will cause my death within a relatively short time, it is my desire that my life not be prolonged by administration of life-sustaining procedures. If my condition is terminal and I am unable to participate in decision regarding my medical treatment, I direct my attending physician to withhold or withdraw procedures that merely prolong the dying process and are not necessary to my comfort or freedom from pain.

Signed this _____ day of _____, 19___.

Signature _____

City, County and State of Residence _____

The declarant is known to me and voluntarily signed this document in my presence.

Witness _____

Address _____

Witness _____

Address _____

KANSAS

NATURAL DEATH ACT

Section 65-28,103

The declaration shall be substantially in the following form, but in addition may include other specific directions.

DECLARATION

Declaration made this ____ day of _____, 19__. I, _____, being of sound mind, willfully and voluntarily make known my desire that my dying shall not be artificially prolonged under the circumstances set forth below, do hereby declare:

If at any time I should have an incurable injury, disease, or illness certified to be a terminal condition by two physicians who have personally examined me, one of whom shall be my attending physician, and the physicians have determined that my death will occur whether or not life-sustaining procedures are utilized and where the application of life-sustaining procedures would serve only to artificially prolong the dying process, I direct that such procedures be withheld or withdrawn, and that I be permitted to die naturally with only the administration of medication or the performance of any medical procedure deemed necessary to provide me with comfort care.

In the absence of my ability to give directions regarding the use of such life-sustaining procedures, it is my intention that this declaration shall be honored by my family and physician(s) as the final expression of my legal right to refuse medical or surgical treatment and accept the consequences from such refusal.

I understand the full import of this declaration and I am emotionally and mentally competent to make this declaration.

Signed _____

City, County and State of Residence _____

The declarant has been personally known to me and I believe him or her to be of sound mind.   I did not sign the declarant's signature above for or at the direction of the declarant. I am not related to the declarant by blood or marriage, entitled to any portion of the estate of the declarant according to the laws of intestate succession or under any will of declarant or codicil thereto, or directly financially responsible for declarant's medical care.

Witness _____
Witness _____

LOUISIANA

DECLARATIONS CONCERNING LIFE-SUSTAINING PROCEDURES

Section 1299.58.3

    The declaration may, but need not, be in the following illustrative form and may include other specific directions.

DECLARATION

    Declaration made this _____ day of _____, 19___.
    I, _____, being of sound mind, willfully and voluntarily make known my desire that my dying shall not be artificially prolonged under the circumstances set forth below and do hereby declare:
    If at any time I should have an incurable injury, disease, or illness certified to be a terminal and irreversible condition by two physicians who have personally examined me, one of whom shall be my attending physician, and the physicians have determined that my death will occur whether or not life-sustaining procedures are utilized and where the application of life-sustaining procedures would serve only to prolong artificially the dying process, I direct that such procedures be withheld or withdrawn and that I be permitted to die naturally with only the administration of medication or the performance of any medical procedure deemed necessary to provide me with comfort care.
    In the absence of my ability to give directions regarding the use of such life-sustaining procedures, it is my intention that this declaration shall be honored by my family and physician(s) as the final expression of my legal right to refuse medical or surgical treatment and accept the consequences from such refusal.
    I understand the full import of this declaration and I am emotionally and mentally competent to make this declaration.

                  Signed _____
City, Parish, and State of Residence _____

    The declarant has been personally known to me and I believe him or her to be of sound mind.

                  Witness _____

                  Witness _____

MAINE

LIVING WILLS

Section 2922

A declaration may, but need not, be in the following form:

DECLARATION

If I should have an incurable or irreversible condition that will cause my death within a short time, and if I am unable to participate in decisions regarding my medical treatment, I direct my attending physician to withhold or withdraw procedures that merely prolong the dying process and are not necessary to my comfort or freedom from pain.

Signed this _____ day of _____, 19___.

                                   Signature _____
City, County, and State of Residence _____

The declarant is known to me and voluntarily signed this document in my presence.

                              Witness _____
                              Address _____

                              Witness _____
                              Address _____

MARYLAND

LIFE-SUSTAINING PROCEDURES

Section 5-602

The declaration shall be substantially in the following form:

DECLARATION

On this _____ day of _____, 19____, I, _____, being of sound mind, willfully and voluntarily direct that my dying shall not be artificially prolonged under the circumstances set forth in this declaration:

If at any time I should have an incurable injury, disease, or illness certified to be a terminal condition by two (2) physicians who have personally examined me, one (1) of whom shall be my attending physician, and the physicians have determined that my death is imminent and will occur whether or not life-sustaining procedures are utilized and where the application of such procedures would serve only to artificially prolong the dying process, I direct that such procedures be withheld or withdrawn, and that I be permitted to die naturally with only the administration of medication, the administration of food and water, and the performance of any medical procedures that is necessary to provide comfort care or alleviate pain. In the absence of my ability to give directions regarding the use of such life-sustaining procedures, it is my intention that this declaration shall be honored by my family and physician(s) as the final expression of my right to control my medical care and treatment.

I am legally competent to make this declaration, and I understand its full import.

```
                              Signed _____
                              Address _____
```

Under penalty of perjury, we state that this declaration was signed by _____ in the presence of the undersigned who, at _____ request, in _____ presence, and in the presence of each other, have hereunto signed our names as witnesses this _____ day of _____, 19___. Further, each of us, individually, states that: The declarant is known to me, and I believe the declarant to be of sound mind. I did not sign the declarant's signature to this declaration. Based upon information and belief, I am not related to the declarant by blood or marriage, a creditor of the declarant, entitled to any portion of the estate of the declarant under any existing testamentary instrument of the declarant, entitled to any financial benefit by reason of the death of the declarant, financially or otherwise responsible for the declarant's medical care, nor an employee of any such person or institution.

```
Witness: _____     Witness: _____
Address: _____     Address: _____
```

MINNESOTA

LIVING WILL - ADULT HEALTH CARE DECISION

Section 4 [145B.04]

A declaration executed after August 1, 1989, under this chapter must be substantially in the form in this section.

HEALTH CARE DECLARATION

Notice:

This is an important legal document. Before signing this document, you should know these important facts:

(a) This document gives your health care providers or your designated proxy the power and guidance to make health care decision according to your wishes when you are in a terminal condition and cannot do so. This document may include what kind of treatment you want or do not want and under what circumstances you want these decisions to be made. You may state where you want or do not want to receive any treatment.

(b) If you name a proxy in this document and that person agrees to serve as your proxy, that person has a duty to act consistently with your wishes. If the proxy does not know your wishes, the proxy has the duty to act in your best interests. If you do not name a proxy, your health care providers have a duty to act consistently with your instructions or tell you that they are unwilling to do so.

(c) This document will remain valid and in effect until and unless you amend or revoke it. Review this document periodically to make sure it continues to reflect your preferences. You may amend or revoke the declaration at any time by notifying your health care providers.

(d) Your named proxy has the same right as you have to examine your medical records and to consent to their disclosure for purposes related to your health care or insurance unless you limit this right in this document.

(e) If there is anything in this document that you do not understand, you should ask for professional help to have it explained to you.

TO MY FAMILY, DOCTORS, AND ALL THOSE CONCERNED WITH MY CARE:

I, _____, being an adult of sound mind, willfully and voluntarily make this statement as a directive to be followed if I am in a terminal condition and become unable to participate in decisions regarding my health care. I understand that my health care providers are legally bound to act consistently with my wishes, within the limits of reasonable medical practice and other applicable law. I also understand that I have the right to make medical and health care decisions for myself as long as I am able to do so and to revoke this declaration at any time.

(1) The following are my feelings and wishes regarding my health care (you may state the circumstances under which this declaration applies): _____
_____
_____

(2) I particularly want to have all appropriate health care that will help in the following ways (you may give instructions for care you do want): _____
_____
_____

(3) I particularly do not want the following (you may list specific treatment you do not want in certain circumstances):
_____
_____

(4) I particularly want to have the following kinds of life-sustaining treatment if I am diagnosed to have a terminal condition (you may list the specific types of life-sustaining treatment that you do want if you have a terminal condition):_____
_____
_____

(5) I particularly do not want the following kinds of life-sustaining treatment if I am diagnosed to have a terminal condition (you may list the specific types of life-sustaining treatment that you do not want if you have a terminal condition):_____
_____
_____

(6) I recognize that if I reject artificially administered sustenance, then I may die of dehydration or malnutrition rather than from my illness or injury. The following are my feelings and wishes regarding artificially administered sustenance should I have a terminal condition (you may indicate whether you wish to receive food and fluids given to you in some other way than by mouth if you have a terminal condition):_____
_____
_____

(7) Thoughts I feel are relevant to my instruction. (You may, but need not, give you religious beliefs, philosophy, or other personal values that you feel are important. You may also state preferences concerning the location of your care.) _____
_____
_____

(8) Proxy Designation. (If you wish, you may name someone to see that your wishes are carried out, but you do not have to do this. You may also name a proxy without including specific instructions regarding your care. If you name a proxy, you should discuss your wishes with that person).

113

If I become unable to communicate my instruction, I designate the following person(s) to act on my behalf consistently with my instruction, if any, as stated in this document. Unless I write instruction that limit my proxy's authority, my proxy has full power and authority to make health care decisions for me. If a guardian or conservator of the person is to be appointed for me, I nominate my proxy named in this document to act as guardian or conservator of my person.

Name: _____

Address: _____

Phone: _____

Relationship (if any): _____

If the person I have named above refuses or is unable or unavailable to act on my behalf, or if I revoke that person's authority to act as my proxy, I authorize the following person to do so:

Name: _____

Address: _____

Phone: _____

Relationship (if any): _____

I understand that I have the right to revoke the appointment of the persons named above to act on my behalf at any time by communicating that decision to the proxy or my health care provider.

Date: _____

Signed: _____

State: _____

County: _____

Subscribed, sworn to, and acknowledge before me by _____ on this _____ day of _____, 19____.

                    _____
                    Notary Public

                            OR

(Sign and date here in the presence of two adult witnesses, neither of whom is entitled to any part of your estate under a will or by operation of law, and neither of whom is your proxy.)

I certify that the declarant voluntarily signed this declaration in my presence and that the declarant is personally known to me. I am not named as a proxy by the declaration, and to the best of my knowledge, I am not entitled to any part of the estate of the declarant under a will or by operation of law.

Witness: _____   Witness: _____

Address: _____   Address: _____

114

MISSISSIPPI

WITHDRAWAL OF LIFE-SAVING MECHANISMS

Section 41-14-107

The execution of the declaration by the declarant shall be in substantially the following form:

DECLARATION made on the _____ day of _____, 19____, by
_____ of _____ (address), _____
(social security number).

I, _____, being of sound mind, declare that if at any time I should suffer a terminal physical condition which causes me severe distress or unconsciousness, and my physician, with the concurrence of two (2) other physicians, believes that there is no expectation of my regaining consciousness or a state of health that is meaningful to me and but for the use of life-sustaining mechanisms my death would be imminent, I desire that the mechanisms be withdrawn so that I may die naturally. However, if I have been diagnosed as pregnant and that diagnosis is known to my physician, this declaration shall have no force or effect during the course of my pregnancy. I further declare that this declaration shall be honored by my family and my physician as the final expression of my desires concerning the manner in which I die.

SIGNED _____

I hereby witness this declaration and attest that:

(1) I personally know the Declaration and believe the Declarant to be of sound mind.
(2) To the best of my knowledge, at the time of the execution of this declaration, I:
(a) Am not related to the Declarant by blood or marriage,
(b) Do not have any claim on the estate of the Declarant,
(c) Am not entitled to any portion of the Declarant's estate by any will or by operation of law, and
(d) Am not a physician attending the Declarant or a person employed by a physician attending the Declarant.

WITNESS _____
ADDRESS _____
SS NO. _____

WITNESS _____
ADDRESS _____
SS NO. _____

MISSOURI

DECLARATIONS, LIFE SUPPORT

Section 459.015(3)

The declaration may be in the following form:

DECLARATION

I have the primary right to make my own decisions concerning treatment that might unduly prolong the dying process. By this declaration I express to my physician, family and friends my intent. If I should have a terminal condition it is my desire that my dying not be prolonged by administration of death-prolonging procedures. If my condition is terminal and I am unable to participate in decisions regarding my medical treatment, I direct my attending physician to withhold or withdraw medical procedures that merely prolong the dying process and are not necessary to my comfort or to alleviate pain. It is not my intent to authorize affirmative or deliberate acts or omissions to shorten my life rather only to permit the natural process of dying.

Signed this _____ day of _____, 19___.

Signature _____

City, County, and State of Residence _____

The declarant is known to me, is eighteen years of age or older, of sound mind and voluntarily signed this document in my presence.

Witness _____
Address _____

Witness _____
Address _____

REVOCATION PROVISION

I hereby revoke the above declaration.

Signed _____
Date _____

MONTANA

LIVING WILL ACT

Section 50-9-103

A declaration directing a physician to withhold or withdraw life-sustaining treatment may, but need not, be in the following form:

DECLARATION

If I should have an incurable or irreversible condition that without the administration of life-sustaining treatment will cause my death within a relatively short time and I am no longer able to make decisions regarding my medical treatment, I direct my attending physician, pursuant to the Montana Rights of the Terminally Ill Act to withhold or withdraw treatment that only prolongs the process of dying and is not necessary to my comfort or to alleviate pain.

Signed this _____ day of _____, 19___.

Signature _____

City, County, and State of Residence _____

The declarant voluntarily signed this document in my presence.

Witness _____
Address _____

Witness _____
Address _____

WITHHOLDING OR WITHDRAWAL OF LIFE-SUSTAINING PROCEDURES

Section 449.610

The declaration shall be in substantially the following form:

DIRECTIVE TO PHYSICIANS

Date _____

I, _____, being of sound mind, intentionally and voluntarily declare:

1. If at any time I am in a terminal condition and become comatose or am otherwise rendered incapable of communicating with my attending physician, and my death is imminent because of an incurable disease, illness or injury, I direct that life-sustaining procedures be withheld or withdrawn, and that I be permitted to die naturally.

2. It is my intention that this directive be honored by my family and attending physician as the final expression of my legal right to refuse medical or surgical treatment and to accept the consequences of my refusal.

3. If I have been found to be pregnant, and that fact is known to my physician, this directive is void during the course of my pregnancy. I understand the full import of this directive, and I am emotionally and mentally competent to execute it.

Signed _____

City, County, and State of Residence _____

The declarant has been personally known to me and I believe _____ to be of sound mind.

Witness _____

Witness _____

NEW HAMPSHIRE

TERMINAL CARE DOCUMENT

Section 137-H:3

The document may be, but need not be, in form and substance substantially as follows:

DECLARATION

Declaration made this _____ day of _____, 19___. I, _____, being of sound mind, willfullly and voluntarily make known my desire that my dying shall not be artificially prolonged under the circumstances set forth below, do hereby declare:

If at any time I should have an incurable injury, disease, or illness certified to be a terminal condition by 2 physicians who have personally examined me, one of whom shall be my attending physician, and the physicians have determined that my death will occur whether or not life-sustaining procedures are utilized and where the application of life-sustaining procedures would serve only to artificially prolong the dying process, I direct that such procedures be withheld or withdrawn, and that I be permitted to die naturally with only the administration of medication, sustenance, or the performance of any medical procedure deemed necessary to provide me with comfort care.

In the absence of my ability to give directions regarding the use of such life-sustaining procedures, it is my intention that this declaration shall be honored by my family and physicians as the final expression of my right to refuse medical or surgical treatment and accept the consequences of such refusal.

I understand the full import of this declaration, and I am emotionally and mentally competent to make this declaration.

Signed _____

State of _____

County of _____

We, the declarant and witnesses, being duly sworn each declare to the notary public or justice of the peace or other official signing below as follows:

1. The declarant signed the instrument as a free and voluntary act of the purposes expressed, or expressly directed another to sign for him.

2. Each witness signed at the request of the declarant, in his presence, and in the presence of the other witness.

3. To the best of my knowledge, at the time of the signing the declarant was at least 18 years of age, and was of sane mind and under no constraint or undue influence.

Declarant _____

Witness _____

Witness _____

The affidavit shall be made before a notary public or justice of the peace or other official authorized to administer oaths in the place of execution, who shall not also serve as a witness, and who shall complete and sign a certificate in content and form substantially as follows:

Sworn to and signed before my by _____, declarant and _____ and _____, witnesses on this _____ day of _____, 19___.

Signature _____
Official Capacity _____

NEW MEXICO

RIGHT TO DIE

Section 24-7-3

New Mexico's right to die statute does not provide a suggested form, but instead provides the following instructions:

A. An individual of sound mind and having reached the age of majority may execute a document directing that if he is ever certified under the Right to Die Act [24-7-1 to 24-7-10 NMSA 1978] as suffering from a terminal illness or being in an irreversible coma, maintenance medical treatment shall not be utilized for the prolongation of his life.

B. A document described in Subsection A of this section is not valid unless it has been executed with the same formalities as required of a valid will pursuant to the provisions of the Probate Code.

NEW YORK

ORDERS NOT TO RESUSCITATE

At the time this book went to press, New York did not have a living will statute. However, a so-called "health-care proxy" bill was under consideration and is expected to pass the New York Legislature. Check with your personal attorney or your local law library for an update on current New York law. In April of 1988, New York did pass an act entitled "Orders Not To Resuscitate", Public Health Law, Section 2960, which addresses the procedures and conditions required to refuse cardiopulmonary resuscitation. Suggested reading if you live in New York, Living Wills in New York: Are They Valid? 38 Syracuse L. Rev. 1369 (1987).

RIGHT TO NATURAL DEATH; BRAIN DEATH

Section 90-321

The following form is specifically determined to meet the requirements above:

DECLARATION OF A DESIRE FOR A NATURAL DEATH

"I, _____, being of sound mind, desire that my life not be prolonged by extraordinary means if my condition is determined to be terminal and incurable. I am aware and understand that this writing authorizes a physician to withhold or discontinue extraordinary means.
     "This the _____ day of _____, 19___.

                              Signature _____

"I hereby state that the declarant, _____, being of sound mind signed the above declaration in my presence and that I am not related to the declarant by blood or marriage and that I do not know or have a reasonable expectation that I would be entitled to any portion of the estate of the declarant under any existing will or codicil of the declarant or as an heir under the Intestate Succession Act if the declarant died on this date without a will. I also state that I am not the declarant's attending physician or an employee of the declarant's attending physician, or an employee of a health facility in which the declarant is a patient or an employee of a nursing home or any group-care home where the declarant resides. I further state that I do not now have any claim against the declarant.

                              Witness _____
                              Witness _____

The clerk or the assistant clerk, or a notary public may, upon proper proof, certify the declaration as follows:

CERTIFICATE

"I, _____, Clerk (Assistant Clerk) of Superior Court of Notary Public (circle one) for _____ County hereby certify that _____, the declarant, appeared before me and swore to me and to the witnesses in my presence that this instrument is his Declaration

Of A Desire For A Natural Death, and that he had willingly and voluntarily made and executed it as his free act and deed for the purposes expressed in it.

"I further certify that _____ and _____, witnesses, appeared before me and swore that they witnessed _____, declarant, sign the attached declaration, believing him to be of sound mind; and also swore that at the time they witnessed the declaration (i) they were not related within the third degree to the declarant or to the declarant's spouse, and (ii) they did not know or have a reasonable expectation that they would be entitled to any portion of the estate of the declarant upon the declarant's death under any will of the declarant or codicil thereto then existing or under the Intestate Succession Act as it provides at that time, and (iii) they were not a physician attending the declarant or an employee of an attending physician or an employee of a health facility in which the declarant was a patient or an employee or a nursing home or any group-care home in which the declarant resided, and (iv) they did not have a claim against the declarant. I further certify that I am satisfied as to the genuineness and due execution of the declaration.

This the _____ day of _____, 19___.

_____
Clerk (Assistant Clerk) of Superior Court
or Notary Public (circle one) for the
County of _____

NORTH DAKOTA

UNIFORM RIGHTS OF TERMINALLY ILL ACT

Section 23-06.4-03

A declaration to withdraw or withhold life-prolonging treatment must be substantially in the following form:

Declaration made this _____ day of _____, 19___.
I, _____, being at least eighteen years of age and of sound mind, willfully and voluntarily make known my desire that my life must not be artificially prolonged under the circumstances set forth below, and do hereby declare:

1. If at any time I should have an incurable condition caused by injury, disease, or illness certified to be a terminal condition to two physicians, and where the application of life-prolonging treatment would serve only to artificially prolong the process of my dying and my attending physician determines that my death is imminent whether or not life-prolonging treatment is utilized, I direct that such treatment be withheld or withdrawn, and that I be permitted to die naturally.

2. In the absence of my ability to give directions regarding the use of such life-prolonging treatment, it is my intention that this declaration be honored by my family and physicians as the final expression of my legal right to refuse medical or surgical treatment and accept the consequences of that refusal, which is death.

3. If I have been diagnosed as pregnant and that diagnosis is known to my physician, this declaration is not effective during the course of my pregnancy.

4. I understand the full import of this declaration and I am emotionally and mentally competent to make this declaration.

5. I understand that I may revoke this declaration at any time.

Signed _____
City, County, and State of Residence _____

The declarant has been personally known to me and I believe the Declarant to be of sound mind. I am not related to the declarant by blood or marriage, nor would I be entitled to any portion of the declarant's estate upon the declarant's death. I am not the declarant's attending physician, a person who has a claim against any portion of the declarant's estate upon the declarant's death, or a person directly financially responsible for the declarant's medical care.

Witness _____

Witness _____

OKLAHOMA

UNIFORM RIGHTS OF THE TERMINALLY ILL ACT

Section 3103(D)

The directive shall be substantially in the following form:

DIRECTIVE TO PHYSICIANS

Directive made this _____ day of _____, 19___.

I, _____, being of sound mind and twenty-one (21) years of age or older, willfully and voluntarily make known my desire that my life shall not be artificially prolonged under the circumstances set forth below, and do hereby declare:

1. If at any time I should have an incurable irreversible condition caused by injury, disease, or illness certified to be a terminal condition by two physicians, I direct that life-sustaining procedures be withheld or withdrawn and that I be permitted to die naturally, if the application of life-sustaining procedures would serve only to artificially prolong the moment of my death and my attending physician determines that my death is imminent whether or not life-sustaining procedures are utilized;

2. In the absence of my ability to give directions regarding the use of such life-sustaining procedures, it is my intention that this directive shall be honored by my family and physicians as the final expression of my legal right to refuse medical or surgical treatment and accept the consequences of such refusal;

3. If I have been diagnosed as pregnant and that diagnosis is known to my physician, this directive shall have no force or effect during the course of my pregnancy;

4. I have been diagnosed and notified as having a terminal condition by _____, M.D. or D.O., whose address is _____, and whose telephone number is _____. I understand that if I have not filled in the name and address of the physician, it shall be presumed that I did not have a terminal condition when I made out this directive;

5. This directive shall be in effect until it is revoked;

6. I understand the full import of this directive and I am emotionally and mentally competent to make this directive; and

7. I understand that I may revoke this directive at any time.

Signed _____
City, County, and State of Residence _____

The declarant has been personally known to me and I believe said declarant to be of sound mind. I am twenty-one (21) years of age or older, I am not related to the declarant by blood or marriage, nor would I be entitled to any portion of the estate of the declarant upon the death of said declarant, nor am I the attending physician of the declarant or an employee of the attending physician or a health care facility in which the declarant is a patient, or a patient in the health care facility in which the declarant is a patient, nor am I financially responsible for the medical care of the declarant, or any person who has a claim against any portion of the estate of the declarant upon the death of the declarant.

Witness _____

Witness _____

STATE OF OKLAHOMA   )
                     : ss.
County of _____   )

    Before me, the undersigned authority, on this day personally appeared _____, (declarant), _____, (witness) and _____, (witness) whose names are subscribed to the foregoing instrument in their respective capacities, and, all of said persons being by me duly sworn, the declarant declared to me and to the said witnesses in my presence that said instrument is his or her "Directive to Physicians", and that the declarant had willingly and voluntarily made and executed it as the free act and deed of the declarant for the purposes therein expressed.
    The foregoing instrument was acknowledged before me this _____ day of _____, 19___.

Signed _____
Notary Public in and for _____
County, Oklahoma

My Commission Expires _____ day of _____, 19___.

RIGHTS WITH RESPECT TO TERMINAL ILLNESS

Section 97.055

The directive shall be in the following form:

DIRECTIVE TO PHYSICIANS

Directive made this _____ day of _____, 19___. I, _____, being of sound mind, wilfully and voluntarily make known my desire that my life shall not be artificially prolonged under the circumstances set forth below and do hereby declare:

1. If at any time I should have an incurable injury, disease or illness certified to be a terminal condition by two physicians, one of whom is the attending physician, and where the application of life-sustaining procedures would serve only to artificially prolong the moment of my death and where my physician determines that my death is imminent whether or not life-sustaining procedures are utilized, I direct that such procedures be withheld or withdrawn, and that I be permitted to die naturally.

2. In the absence of my ability to give directions regarding the use of such life-sustaining procedures, it is my intention that this directive shall be honored by my family and physician(s) as the final expression of my legal right to refuse medical or surgical treatment and accept the consequences from such refusal.

3. I understand the full import of this directive and I am emotionally and mentally competent to make this directive.

Signed _____
City, County, and State of Residence _____

I hereby witness this directive and attest that:

(1) I personally know the Declarant and believe the Declarant to be of sound mind.

(2) To the best of my knowledge, at the time of the execution of this directive, I:

(a) Am not related to the Declarant by blood or marriage,

(b) Do not have any claim on the estate of the Declarant,

(c) Am not entitled to any portion of the Declarant's estate by any will or by operation of law, and

(d) Am not a physician attending the Declarant, a person employed by a physician attending the Declarant or a person employed by a health facility in which the Declarant is a patient.

(3) I understand that if I have not witnessed this directive in good faith I may be responsible for any damages that arise out of giving this directive its intended effect.

Witness: _____   Witness: _____

DEATH WITH DIGNITY ACT

Section 44-77-50

The declaration must be substantially in the following form with the procedure and requirements for revocation of the declaration appearing either in boldface print or in all upper case letters, the characters in either case being of at least the same size as used in the rest of the declaration:

STATE OF SOUTH CAROLINA
DECLARATION OF A DESIRE FOR A NATURAL DEATH
COUNTY OF _____

I, _____, being at least eighteen years of age and a resident of and domiciled in the City of _____, County of _____, State of South Carolina, make this Declaration this _____ day of _____, 19___.
I wilfully and voluntarily make known my desire that no life-sustaining procedures be used to prolong my dying if my condition is terminal and I declare:
If at any time I have a condition certified to be a terminal condition by two physicians who have personally examined me, one of whom is my attending physician, and the physicians have determined that my death will occur within a relatively short period of time without the use of life-sustaining procedures and where the application of life-sustaining procedures would serve only to prolong the dying process, I direct that the procedures be withheld or withdrawn, and that I be permitted to die naturally with only the administration of medication or the performance of any medical procedure necessary to provide me with comfort care.
In the absence of my ability to give directions regarding the use of life-sustaining procedures, it is my intention that this Declaration be honored by my family and physicians and any health facility in which I may be a patient as the final expression of my legal right to refuse medical or surgical treatment, and I accept the consequences from the refusal.
I am aware that this Declaration authorizes a physician to withhold or withdraw life-sustaining procedures. I am emotionally and mentally competent to make this Declaration.

THIS DECLARATION MAY BE REVOKED:

(1) BY BEING DEFACED, TORN, OBLITERATED, OR OTHERWISE DESTROYED, IN EXPRESSION OF THE DECLARANT'S INTENT TO REVOKE, BY THE DECLARANT OR BY SOME PERSON IN THE PRESENCE OF AND BY THE DIRECTION OF THE DECLARANT. REVOCATION BY DESTRUCTION OF ONE OR MORE OF MULTIPLE ORIGINAL DECLARATIONS REVOKES ALL OF THE ORIGINAL DECLARATIONS. THE REVOCATION OF THE ORIGINAL DECLARATIONS ACTUALLY NOT DESTROYED BECOMES

EFFECTIVE ONLY UPON COMMUNICATION TO THE ATTENDING PHYSICIAN. THE ATTENDING PHYSICIAN SHALL RECORD IN THE DECLARANT'S MEDICAL RECORD THE TIME AND DATE WHEN THE PHYSICIAN RECEIVED NOTIFICATION OF THE REVOCATION;

(2) BY A WRITTEN REVOCATION SIGNED AND DATED BY THE DECLARANT EXPRESSING HIS INTENT TO REVOKE. THE REVOCATION BECOMES EFFECTIVE ONLY UPON COMMUNICATION TO THE ATTENDING PHYSICIAN. THE ATTENDING PHYSICIAN SHALL RECORD IN THE DECLARANT'S MEDICAL RECORD THE TIME AND DATE WHEN THE PHYSICIAN RECEIVED NOTIFICATION OF THE WRITTEN REVOCATION;

(3) BY AN ORAL EXPRESSION BY THE DECLARANT OF HIS INTENT TO REVOKE THE DECLARATION. THE REVOCATION BECOMES EFFECTIVE ONLY UPON COMMUNICATION TO THE ATTENDING PHYSICIAN BY THE DECLARANT. HOWEVER, AN ORAL REVOCATION MADE BY THE DECLARANT BECOMES EFFECTIVE UPON COMMUNICATION TO THE ATTENDING PHYSICIAN BY A PERSON OTHER THAN THE DECLARANT IF:

(a) THE PERSON WAS PRESENT WHEN THE ORAL REVOCATION WAS MADE;
(b) THE REVOCATION WAS COMMUNICATED TO THE PHYSICIAN WITHIN A REASONABLE TIME;
(c) THE PHYSICAL OR MENTAL CONDITION OF THE DECLARANT MAKES IT IMPOSSIBLE FOR THE PHYSICIAN TO CONFIRM THROUGH SUBSEQUENT CONVERSATION WITH THE DECLARANT THAT THE REVOCATION HAS OCCURRED.

THE ATTENDING PHYSICIAN SHALL RECORD IN THE PATIENT'S MEDICAL RECORD THE TIME, DATE, AND PLACE OF THE REVOCATION AND THE TIME, DATE, AND PLACE, IF DIFFERENT, OF WHEN HE RECEIVED NOTIFICATION OF THE REVOCATION. TO BE EFFECTIVE AS A REVOCATION, THE ORAL EXPRESSION CLEARLY MUST INDICATE A DESIRE THAT THE DECLARATION NOT BE GIVEN EFFECT OR THAT LIFE-SUSTAINING PROCEDURES BE ADMINISTERED;

(4) BY A WRITTEN, SIGNED, AND DATED REVOCATION OR AN ORAL REVOCATION BY A PERSON DESIGNATED BY THE DECLARANT IN THE DECLARATION, EXPRESSING THE DESIGNEE'S INTENT PERMANENTLY OR TEMPORARILY TO REVOKE THE DECLARATION. THE REVOCATION BECOMES EFFECTIVE ONLY UPON COMMUNICATION TO THE ATTENDING PHYSICIAN BY THE DESIGNEE. THE ATTENDING PHYSICIAN SHALL RECORD IN THE DECLARANT'S MEDICAL RECORD THE TIME, DATE, AND PLACE OF THE REVOCATION AND THE TIME, DATE, AND PLACE, IF DIFFERENT, OF WHEN THE PHYSICIAN RECEIVED NOTIFICATION OF THE REVOCATION. A DESIGNEE MAY REVOKE ONLY IF THE DECLARANT IS INCOMPETENT TO DO SO. IF THE DECLARANT WISHES TO DESIGNATE A PERSON WITH AUTHORITY TO REVOKE THIS DECLARATION ON HIS BEHALF, THE NAME AND ADDRESS OF THAT PERSON MUST BE ENTERED BELOW:

THIS DECLARATION ON HIS BEHALF, THE NAME AND ADDRESS OF THAT PERSON MUST BE ENTERED BELOW:

_____
NAME OF DESIGNEE

_____
ADDRESS

_____
Declarant

STATE OF _____   AFFIDAVIT
COUNTY OF _____

We, _____ and _____, the undersigned witnesses to the
foregoing Declaration, dated the _____ day of _____, 19___, being
first duly sworn, declare to the undersigned authority, on the basis of
our best information and belief, that the Declaration was on that date
signed by the declarant as and for his DECLARATION OF A DESIRE FOR A
NATURAL DEATH in our presence and we, at his request and in his
presence, and in the presence of each other, subscribe our names as
witnesses on that date. The declarant is personally known to us, and
we believe him to be of sound mind. Each of us affirms that he is
qualified as a witness to this Declaration under the provisions of the
South Carolina Death With Dignity Act in that he is not related to the
declarant by blood or marriage, either as a spouse, lineal ancestor,
descendant of the parents of the declarant, or spouse of any of them;
nor directly financially responsible for the declarant's medical care;
nor entitled to any portion of the declarant's estate upon his decease,
whether under any will or as an heir by intestate succession; nor the
beneficiary of a life insurance policy of the declarant; nor the
declarant's attending physician; nor an employee of the attending
physician; nor a person who has a claim against the declarant's
decedent's estate as of this time. No more than one of use is an
employee of a health facility in which the declarant is a patient. If
the declarant is a patient in a hospital or skilled or intermediate
care nursing facility at the date of execution of this Declaration at
least one of us is an ombudsman designated by the State Ombudsman,
Office of the Governor.

_____
Witness

_____
Witness

Subscribed before me by _____, the declarant, and subscribed
and sworn to before me by _____ and _____, the witnesses,
this _____ day of _____, 19___.

_____
Notary public for _____
My commission expires _____

131

LIVING WILLS

Section 32-11-105

The declaration may be substantially in the following form:

LIVING WILL

I, _____, willfully and voluntarily make known my desire that my dying shall not be artificially prolong under the circumstances set forth below, and do hereby declare:

If at any time I should have a terminal condition and my attending physician has determined that there can be no recovery from such condition and my death is imminent, where the application of life-prolonging procedures would serve only to artificially prolong the dying process, I direct that such procedures be withheld or withdrawn, and that I be permitted to die naturally with only the administration of medications or the performance of any medical procedure deemed necessary to provide me with comfortable care or to alleviate pain.

In the absence of my ability to give directions regarding the use of such life-prolonging procedures, it is my intention that this declaration shall be honored by my family and physician as the final expression of my legal right to refuse medical or surgical treatment and accept the consequences of such refusal.

I understand the full import of this declaration, and I am emotionally and mentally competent to make this declaration. In acknowledgment whereof, I do hereinafter affix my signature on this the _____ day of _____, 19___.

                                    _____
                                    Declarant

We, the subscribing witnesses hereto, are personally acquainted with and subscribe our names hereto at the request of the declarant, an adult, whom we believe to be of sound mind, fully aware of the action taken herein and its possible consequence.
We, the undersigned witnesses, further declare that we are not related to the declarant by blood or marriage; that we are not entitled to any portion of the estate of the declarant upon his decease under

any will or codicil thereto presently existing or by operation of law then existing; that we are not the attending physician, an employee of the attending physician or a health facility in which the declarant is a patient; and that we are not a person who, at the present time, has a claim against any portion of the estate of the declarant upon his death.

_____
Witness

_____
Witness

    Subscribed, sworn to and acknowledged before me by _____, the declarant, and subscribed and sworn to before me by _____ and _____, witnesses, this _____ day of _____, 19___.

_____
Notary Public

NATURAL DEATH

Section 3

A written directive may be in the following form:

DIRECTIVE TO PHYSICIANS

"Directive made this _____ day of _____, 19___.

"I, _____, being of sound mind, willfully and voluntarily make known my desire that my life shall not be artificially prolonged under the circumstances set forth below, and do hereby declare:

"1. If at any time I should have an incurable condition caused by injury, disease, or illness certified to be a terminal condition by two physicians, and where the application of life-sustaining procedures would serve only to artificially prolong the moment of my death and where my attending physician determines that my death is imminent whether or not life-sustaining procedures are utilized, I direct that such procedures be withheld or withdrawn, and that I be permitted to die naturally.

"2. In the absence of my ability to give directions regarding the use of such life-sustaining procedures, it is my intention that this directive shall be honored by my family and physicians as the final expression of my legal right to refuse medical or surgical treatment and accept the consequences from such refusal.

"3. If I have been diagnosed as pregnant and that diagnosis is known to my physician, this directive shall have no force or effect during the course of my pregnancy.

"4. This directive shall be in effect until it is revoked.

"5. I understand the full import of this directive and I am emotionally and mentally competent to make this directive.

"6. I understand that I may revoke this directive at any time.

"Signed _____
City, County, and State of Residence _____

The declarant has been personally known to me and I believe him or her to be of sound mind. I am not related to the declarant by blood or marriage, nor would I be entitled to any portion of the declarant's estate on his decease, nor am I the attending physician of the declarant or an employee of the attending physician or a health facility in which the declarant is a patient, or a patient in the health care facility in which the declarant is a patient, or any person who has a claim against any portion of the estate of the declarant upon his decease.

Witness: _____   Witness: _____

PERSONAL CHOICE AND LIVING WILL ACT

Section 75-2-1104

The directive shall be in substantially the following form:

DIRECTIVE TO PHYSICIANS AND PROVIDERS OF MEDICAL SERVICES

This directive is made this _____ day of _____, 19___.

1. I, _____, being of sound mind, willfully and voluntarily make known my desire that my life not be artificially prolonged by life-sustaining procedures except as I may otherwise provide in this directive.

2. I declare that if at any time I should have an injury, disease, or illness, which is certified in writing to be a terminal condition by two physicians who have personally examined me, and in the opinion of those physicians the application of life-sustaining procedures would serve only to unnaturally prolong the moment of my death and to unnaturally postpone or prolong the dying process, I direct that these procedures be withheld or withdrawn and my death be permitted to occur naturally.

3. I expressly intend this directive to be a final expression of my legal right to refuse medical or surgical treatment and to accept the consequences from this refusal which shall remain in effect notwithstanding my future inability to give current medical directions to treating physicians and other providers of medical services.

4. I understand that the term "life-sustaining procedure" does not include the administration of medication or sustenance, or the performance of any medical procedure deemed necessary to provide comfort care, or to alleviate pain, except to the extent I specify below that any of these procedures be considered life-sustaining.

5. I reserve the right to give current medical directions to physicians and other providers of medical services so long as I am able, even though these directions may conflict with the above written directive that life-sustaining procedures be withheld or withdrawn.

6. I understand the full import of this directive and declare that I am emotionally and mentally competent to make this directive.

```
                     _____
                     Declarant's signature
City, County, and State of Residence _____
```

We witnesses certify that each of us is 18 years of age or older and each personally witnessed the declarant sign or direct the signing of this directive; that we are acquainted with the declarant and believe him to be of sound mind; that the declarant's desires are as expressed above; that neither of us is a person who signed the above directive on behalf of the declarant; that we are not related to the declarant by blood or marriage nor are we entitled to any portion of declarant's estate according to the laws of intestate succession of this state or under any will or codicil of declarant; that we are not directly financially responsible for declarant's medical care; and that we are not agents of any health care facility in which the declarant may be a patient at the time of signing this directive.

_____
Witness
_____
Address

_____
Witness
_____
Address

VERMONT

TERMINAL CARE DOCUMENT

Section 5253

The document may, but need not, be in form and substance substantially as follows:

"To my family, my physician, my lawyer, my clergyman. To any medical facility in whose care I happen to be. To any individual who may become responsible for my health, welfare or affairs.

"Death is as much a reality as birth, growth, maturity and old age - it is the one certainty of life. If the time comes when I, _____, can no longer take part in decisions of my own future, let this statement stand as an expression of my wishes, while I am still of sound mind.

"If the situation should arise in which I am in a terminal state and there is no reasonable expectation of my recovery, I direct that I be allowed to die a natural death and that my life not be prolonged by extraordinary measure. I do, however, ask that medication be mercifully administered to me to alleviate suffering even though this may shorten my remaining life.

"This statement is made after careful consideration and is in accordance with my strong convictions and beliefs. I want the wishes and directions here expressed carried out to the extent permitted by law. Insofar as they are not legally enforceable, I hope that those to whom this will is addressed will regard themselves as morally bound by these provisions.

Signed: _____
Date: _____

Witness: _____
Witness: _____

Copies of this request have been given to:

_____
_____
_____

VIRGINIA

NATURAL DEATH ACT

Section 54.1-2984

A declaration may, but need not, be in one of the following forms:

Declaration made this _____ day of _____, 19___. I, _____, willfully and voluntarily make known my desire and do hereby declare:

CHOSE ONLY ONE OF THE NEXT TWO PARAGRAPHS AND CROSS THROUGH THE OTHER

If at any time I should have a terminal condition and my attending physician has determined that there can be no recovery from such condition, my death is imminent, and I am comatose, incompetent or otherwise mentally or physically incapable of communication, I designate _____ to make a decision on by behalf as to whether life prolonging procedures shall be withheld or withdrawn. In the event that my designee decides that such procedures should be withheld or withdrawn, I wish to be permitted to die naturally with only the administration of medication or the performance of any medical procedure deemed necessary to provide me with comfort care or to alleviate pain.

OR

If at any time I should have a terminal condition and my attending physician has determined that there can be no recovery from such condition and my death is imminent, where the application of life-prolonging procedures would serve only to artificially prolong the dying process, I direct that such procedures be withheld or withdrawn, and that I be permitted to die naturally with only the administration of medication or the performance of any medical procedure deemed necessary to provide me with comfort care or to alleviate pain.

In the absence of my ability to give directions regarding the use of such life-prolonging procedures, it is my intention that this declaration shall be honored by my family and physician as the final expression of my legal right to reuse medical or surgical treatment and accept the consequences of such refusal.

I understand the full import of this declaration and I am emotionally and mentally competent to make this declaration.

_____
Signed

The declarant is known to me and I believe him or her to be of sound mind.

_____
Witness

_____
Witness

WASHINGTON

NATURAL DEATH ACT

Section 70.122.030

The directive shall be essentially in the following form:

DIRECTIVE TO PHYSICIANS

Directive made this _____ day of _____, 19___.

I, _____, being of sound mind, wilfully, and voluntarily make known my desire that my life shall not be artificially prolonged under the circumstances set forth below, and do hereby declare that:

(a) If at any time I should have an incurable injury, disease, or illness certified to be a terminal condition by two physicians, and where the application of life-sustaining procedures would serve only to artificially prolong the moment of my death and where my physician determines that my death is imminent whether or not life-sustaining procedures are utilized, I direct that such procedures be withheld or withdrawn, and that I be permitted to die naturally.

(b) In the absence of my ability to give directions regarding the use of such life-sustaining procedures, it is my intention that this directive shall be honored by my family and physician(s) as the final expression of my legal right to refuse medical or surgical treatment and I accept the consequences from such refusal.

(c) If I have been diagnosed as pregnant and that diagnosis is known to my physician, this directive shall have no force or effect during the course of my pregnancy.

(d) I understand the full import of this directive and I am emotionally and mentally competent to make this directive.

Signed _____

City, County, and State of Residence _____

The declarer has been personally known to me and I believe him or her to be of sound mind.

Witness _____

Witness _____

WEST VIRGINIA

NATURAL DEATH ACT

Section 16-30-3

The declaration shall be substantially in the following form:

DECLARATION

"Declaration made this _____ day of _____, 19___. I, _____, being of sound mind, willfully and voluntarily make known my desires that my dying shall not be artificially prolonged under the circumstances set forth below, do declare:

"If at any time I should have an incurable injury, disease or illness certified to be a terminal condition by two physicians who have personally examined me, one of whom is my attending physician, and the physicians have determined that my death will occur whether or not life-sustaining procedures are utilized and where the application of life-sustaining procedures would serve only to artificially prolong the dying process, I direct that such procedures be withheld or withdrawn, and that I be permitted to die naturally with only the administration of nutrition, medication or the performance of any medical procedure deemed necessary to provide me with comfort, care or to alleviate pain.

"In the absence of my ability to give directions regarding the use of such life-sustaining procedures, it is my intention that this declaration be honored by my family and physician(s) as the final expression of my legal right to refuse medical or surgical treatment and accept the consequences resulting from such refusal.

"I understand the full import of this declaration and I am emotionally and mentally competent to make this declaration.

"Signed _____
"Address _____

"I did not sign the declarant's signature above for or at the direction of the declarant. I am at least eighteen years of age and am not related to the declarant by blood or marriage, entitled to any portion of the estate of the declarant according to he laws of intestate succession of the State of West Virginia or to the best of my knowledge under any will of declarant or codicil thereto, or directly financially responsible for declarant's medical care. I am not the declarant's attending physician, an employee of the attending physician, nor an employee of the health facility in which the declarant is a patient.

"Witness _____

"Witness _____

"STATE OF _____,
"County of _____, to-wit:

"This day personally appeared before me, the undersigned authority, a Notary Public in and for _____ County, _____ (State), _____ (witness) and _____ (witness) who, being first duly sworn, say that they are the subscribing witnesses to the declaration of _____ (declarant), which declaration is dated the ____ day of _____, 19___; and that on the said date the said _____ (declarant), the declarant, signed, sealed, published and declared the same as and for his declaration, in the presence of both these affiants; and that these affiants, at the request of said declarant, in the presence of each other, and in the presence of said declarant, all present at the same time, signed their names as attesting witnesses to said declaration.

"Affiants further say that this affidavit is made at the request of _____ (declarant), declarant, and in his presence, and that _____ (declarant), at the time the declaration was executed, was in the opinion of affiants, of sound mind and memory, and over the age of eighteen years.

_____

_____

"Taken, subscribed and sworn to before me by _____ (witness) and _____ (witness) this ____ day of _____, 19___.

"My commission expires: _____.

_____
Notary Public

142

NATURAL DEATH

Section 154.03

The declaration distributed by the department of health and social services shall be in the following form:

DECLARATION TO PHYSICIANS

Declaration made this _____ day of _____, 19___.

1. I, _____, being of sound mind, wilfully and voluntarily state my desire that my dying may no be artificially prolonged if I have an incurable injury or illness certified to be a terminal condition by 2 physicians who have personally examined me, one of whom is my attending physician, and if the physicians have determined that my death is imminent, so that the application of life-sustaining procedures would serve only to prolong artificially the dying process. Under these circumstances, I direct that life-sustaining procedures be withheld or withdrawn and that I be permitted to die naturally, with only:

    a. The continuation of nutritional support and fluid maintenance; and

    b. The alleviation of pain by administering medication or other medical procedure.

2. If I am unable to give directions regarding the use of life-sustaining procedures, I intend that my family and physician honor this declaration as the final expression of my legal right to refuse medical or surgical treatment and to accept the consequences from this refusal.

3. If I have been diagnosed as pregnant and my physician knows of this diagnosis, this declaration has no effect during the course of my pregnancy.

4. This declaration takes effect immediately.

I understand this declaration and I am emotionally and mentally competent to make this declaration.

Signed _____

Address _____

I know the declarant personally and I believe him or her to be of sound mind. I am not related to the declarant by blood or marriage, and am not entitled to any portion of the declarant's estate under any will of the declarant. I am neither the declarant's attending physician, the attending nurse, the attending medical staff nor an employee of the attending physician or of the inpatient health care facility in which the declarant may be a patient and I have no claim against the declarant's estate at this time, except that, if I am not a health care provider who is involved in the medical care of the declarant, I may be an employee of the inpatient health care facility regardless of whether or not the facility may have a claim against the estate of the declarant.

Witness _____

Witness _____

WYOMING

LIVING WILL

Section 35-22-102

The declaration may be substantially in the following form:

DECLARATION

Declaration made this _____ day of _____, 19___. I, _____, being of sound mind, willfully and voluntarily make known my desire that my dying shall not be artificially prolonged under the circumstances set forth below, do hereby declare:

If at any time I should have an incurable injury, disease or other illness certified to be a terminal condition by two (2) physicians who have personally examined me, one (1) of whom shall be my attending physician, and the physicians have determined that my death will occur whether or not life-sustaining procedures are utilized and where the application of life-sustaining procedures would serve only to artificially prolong the dying process, I direct that such procedures be withheld or withdrawn, and that I be permitted to die naturally with only the administration of medication or the performance of any medical procedure deemed necessary to provide me with comfort care. If, in spite of this declaration, I am comatose or otherwise unable to make treatment decisions for myself, I HEREBY designate _____ to make treatment decisions for me.

In the absence of my ability to give directions regarding the use of life-sustaining procedures, it is my intention that this declaration shall be honored by my family and physician(s) and agent as the final expression of my legal right to refuse medical or surgical treatment and accept the consequences from this refusal. I understand the full import of this declaration and I am emotionally and mentally competent to make this declaration.

Signed _____

City, County, and State of Residence _____

The declarant has been personally known to me and I believe him or her to be of sound mind. I did not sign the declarant's signature above for or at the direction of the declarant. I am not related to the declarant by blood or marriage, entitled to any portion of the estate of the declarant according to the laws of intestate succession or under any will of the declarant or codicil thereto, or directly financially responsible for declarant's medical care.

Witness _____

Witness _____

NATURAL DEATH WITH DIGNITY:

PROTECTING YOUR RIGHT TO REFUSE MEDICAL TREATMENT

CHAPTER 5 —

PERSONAL DECLARATION OF INTENT RE: LIMITING CONSENT

From the forms provided in the proceeding chapter, you should now have a reasonable idea of what you want to include or provide in your own personal living will. Also, from a review of these living will statutes, you may also sense an inadequacy or need to go beyond the basic language contained within the various living will statutes.

If you have reached this conclusion, you will want to draft your own personal declaration of intent regarding limiting medical consent, and go beyond the narrow call of the statutory language of the various statutory forms. As you do so, you will be taking a substantial step toward providing clear and convincing evidence of your intent regarding medical consent, in a variety of circumstances.

Your personal declaration of intent regarding limiting medical consent will be based upon the various living will statutes, but will be premised upon your basic fundamental constitutional liberty interest right to refuse medical treatment. Thus, if your State living will statute does not sufficiently grant you discretion to sufficiently limit medical consent, then a declaration should be prepared which goes beyond the limitations contained within the living will statute. As you saw in a review of the state statutes, many states do not require strict adherence to any particular statutory language. As a result, your personal declaration of intent may be incorporated into your statutory living will. In those states that have no statutory living wills, or in those states that limit the language that can be incorporated into a statutory living will, then a second or separate legal instrument may be drafted expressing your intent regarding limiting medical consent so it will be made legally enforceable. Legally enforceable means it needs to be in writing and verified by a form legally acceptable as evidence in your state. This will usually include witnesses to your signature and a notary public, either verifying your signature and/or the signatures of the witnesses. Placing the information in the form of an affidavit may also be recommended. The decision as to precisely what format to follow with what proof or verification, is best left to the professional opinion and advice of an attorney in your state, which you should contact to review your proposed documents.

Even though one of the authors of this book is an attorney, there is still no way to avoid the fact that when you need legal advice, you need to consult with an attorney. Do not use this book as a substitute for contacting an attorney if you do need legal advice. Just as it is good advice to have an attorney review your traditional will addressing the disposition of your property, it likewise makes perfectly good sense to have an attorney review your living will and any additional or different declaration. If you or your attorney need additional information about living wills in your particular state, check the resource section of this book, your state law library, or your state attorney general.

The bottom line: You want your living will and/or personal declaration of intent limiting medical consent to include those conditions under which you would not want to be treated, and to do it in such a manner that it is legally enforceable. The documents you will prepare will have two basic objectives. 1. Your first line of defense is to make these documents available to your health care providers and members of your family so at the appropriate time the undesired medical care will not be provided. 2. If, for some reason, this first line of defense fails and you have care administered to you while you are incompetent that you directed not to be provided, then these properly prepared documents will give your friend or family, through your attorney, the evidence they need to have a court order the offending treatment stopped.

A living will, even one that incorporates a personal declaration of intent regarding limiting medical consent, is anything but a perfect document, and we do not believe having such a document will guarantee you will not receive the treatment you do not want. However, having a living will or a declaration of intent is the only way you will ever have a decent chance of receiving or not receiving the care you desire. Preparing these documents will not guarantee your family members, or your attorney, will not have to go to court to enforce your desires. However, if that unfortunate circumstance becomes necessary, then well drawn up documents will provide physicians, hospital administrators, or judges the "clear and convincing" evidence of what you would be requesting if you were competent to make the request yourself.

For purposes of example, and to help bring this all together for you, the following is a copy of co-author, Lee R. Kerr's personal living will. Although no one can write your living will for you because of its extremely personal nature, you may use Mr. Kerr's living will as a drafting aide. Simply keep in mind the extremely personal nature of a living will and that it must truly reflect your own personal desires, needs and instructions. Also keep in mind Mr. Kerr's will was drafted under the laws of Montana, which permit deviation from the standardized form, so Mr. Kerr's personal declaration of intent regarding limiting medical consent is incorporated into the Montana statutory living will form. Your personal statement of intent may have to be by a separate sworn statement or affidavit if the terms, conditions and instructions you want to give are inconsistent or not permitted under your State Living Will Statute, or your State has no living will statute.

DECLARATION

If I should have an incurable or irreversible condition that will cause my death, it is my desire my life not be prolonged by the administration of life sustaining procedures, including tube nutrition and hydration. If my condition is terminal and I am unable to participate in decisions regarding my medical treatment, I direct my attending physician to withhold or withdraw procedures that merely prolong the dying process and are not necessary to my comfort or my freedom from pain.

It is my intention that this declaration should be valid until revoked by me. I further intend that if any provision of this declaration is ruled invalid, it is my intent that the rest and remainder of the provisions shall be given full force and effect.

This declaration is made after careful consideration and pursuant to my strong conviction and beliefs. I desire and expect my intentions and directions expressed herein to be carried out to the fullest extent permitted by law. As to any provision not legally enforceable, it is my greatest hope that those to whom this declaration is addressed will regard themselves as morally bound to the provisions in any case.

As an attorney, I highly value my cognitive functions and my abilities to interact and communicate. If I should ever lose my ability to communicate with others, or lose the use of my hands and my full cognitive abilities, I would not want to live in that condition. If I should ever be found to have a prognosis of permanent unconsciousness, then I expressly refuse my consent to medical treatment, and direct all life supporting therapies discontinued except for any such treatment intended solely to keep me comfortable while I die. I do not wish to be in pain but would include the withholding of nutrition. I understand it may be necessary for my comfort to continue hydration. These are my wishes and directions if I have a prognosis of permanent unconsciousness, permanently comatose, in an irreversibly vegetative state, persistent vegetative state, or quadriplegic without the ability to communicate either orally or with my hands, and have no reasonable prognosis of regaining the use of my hands or regaining speech.

I realize at some point in my life it may be necessary for my health care or treatment to be placed on a respirator or be tube fed or dialyzed. However, I am willing to receive these treatments only for acute medical conditions and not as a chronic treatment. It is my strongest desire, intentions, and instructions that I do not live my life attached to a machine without the ability to communicate.

I also realize some of the above treatments may be necessary during a period of assessment. I consent to the utilization of the above machines or devices, but only for a reasonable but brief period of assessment. If after assessment it is concluded I do not have a reasonable prognosis of regaining my ability to communicate, I hereby order the withdraw of any medical treatment used to sustain my life, including, but not limited to, the use of a respirator, tube feeding, antibiotics, or dialysis.

Likewise, should I be suffering from a chronic illness, such as a degenerative neurological disease or cancer, and I am beyond any reasonable hope of recovery, I direct all life supporting therapies discontinued. Further, if I am diagnosed as being in a persistent vegetative state, or am in a coma for more than six weeks duration, I direct all life supporting therapies withdrawn, regardless of prognosis or other possible chance of recovery. If I lose my ability to communicate, which I value so highly, and I must submit the most private of my bodily functions to the attention of others, then I no longer wish my physical existence to be maintained. The fact that my physical existence could be maintained for months, years, or decades is abhorrent to me and thus I am directing the withholding of medical treatment and refusing consent to medical treatment or care as outlined above.

This directive is based in part upon Montana's Living Will Act and more broadly upon my Federal and State Constitutional liberty interest right to refuse medical treatment. This document, although executed this date, is intended to be an expression of my wishes, desires, and directives from this date forward until my death unless otherwise revoked.

If anyone treating or caring for me, or the institution for which they are employed refuse to honor this directive, and continue or institute treatment against my will as reflected in this document, I consider such treatment an intentional act of assault, and direct my family to lodge a criminal assault complaint against those involved in violation of my fundamental constitutional right to refuse medical treatment. Further, I direct my family to institute a civil suit against those involved in treating me against my will, seeking general damages and punitive damages for an intentional tort. As an attorney, I regret using saber rattling language to resolve a potential dispute. Yet, if this is the only language understood and responded to, then so be it.

In the same spirit, any health care provider or facility that acts in accordance with the directives contained herein should not be subject to any civil or criminal liability or guilty of any unprofessional conduct.

I fully intend this to be my final expression of my legal right to refuse consent to medical care or treatment, and fully accept the consequences of such refusal. The declaration provided above is my directive and statement of intent regarding being permitted to die naturally with dignity.

Signed this _25_ day of September, 1990.

_____
Lee R. Kerr
Hysham, Treasure County, Montana

The declarant is known to me to be voluntarily signing this document in my presence.

Kathleen Thomas
WITNESS

Valerie J. Cramer
WITNESS

Hysham, MT 59038
ADDRESS

Hysham, MT 59038
ADDRESS

NATURAL DEATH WITH DIGNITY:

PROTECTING YOUR RIGHT TO REFUSE MEDICAL TREATMENT

CHAPTER 6 —

POWER OF ATTORNEY FOR LIMITING MEDICAL CONSENT

You are now at the last step of the process of preparing all the necessary documents. The last document necessary is a durable power of attorney for limiting medical consent. As you may have noticed in the various state living will statutes, some of the separate statutes provided for the appointment of a proxy or a power of attorney for granting or refusing medical consent. If you are from one of these states that provided for a health care proxy, and authorized flexibility in the language contained in the living will, then you will be able to complete all three of the major objectives of this book in one document, the living will.

However, as you have been cautioned previously, do to particular circumstances within the various states, it may not be legally appropriate to accomplish all three tasks within one document. Thus, as indicated previously, it is strongly recommended you consult with an attorney regarding reviewing your actual documents necessary to accomplish these three important goals. Seven states have living will statutes (Delaware, Florida, Louisiana, Texas, Utah, Virginia, and Wyoming) that specifically authorize the appointment of a health care proxy to refuse life sustaining treatment. In addition, the living will statutes of four other states (Hawaii, Idaho, Indiana and Iowa) indirectly authorize such appointments. Further, Several states have recognized the wisdom of providing a pracitical procedure by enacting durable power of attorney statutes that specifically authorize an individual to appoint a surrogate to make medical treatment decisions, (Alaska., Cal., Id., Kan., Me., Nev., Oh., Or., Pa., RI., Tx., Vt.).

Your starting point for this step is an understanding of the basic terminology. A power of attorney is a written document. In it you grant certain powers to another person often referred to as the "attorney in fact" or "power of attorney". This enables the other person to act on your behalf. A power of attorney may be very specific. It can limit the power of the agent to a specific act, such as consenting to or refusing medical care, or it may be very broad and without definition. A simple power of attorney is not valid once you become incapacitated. However, if you have a written durable power of attorney before you become incapacitated, that document will be effective during your disability. A durable power of attorney is a special type of power of attorney because it remains effective even when you become incapacitated. It does not remain effective after your death however. All powers of attorney are terminated upon the death of the principal.

A power of attorney does not have to be given to a lawyer. However, your power of attorney should be someone who knows you very well. Obviously, this is the person who is going to be making important decisions for you. The person you grant the power of attorney to has to carry out your wishes and always act with your best interests in mind. The person you designate may be a relative, a close friend, your personal attorney, or someone you trust. If there is no one you trust with this power, it would be recommended you do not draft a power of attorney. The laws that provide for durable powers of attorney vary between the states. All fifty states have power of attorney statutes of one form or another. Thus, you should consult with an attorney to insure your durable power of attorney complies with your state's requirements. The power of attorney is also something that must be prepared in advance. If you do not prepare a power of attorney while you are competent, it will be too late once your competency comes into question.

A durable general power of attorney is usually used to handle financial and property issues. By language contained within a durable general power of attorney, it is usually indicated that the person granted the power of attorney can do any and all things the principal would be legally authorized to do if competent. In some of these states, a durable general power of attorney is sufficiently broad enough to also make health care decisions for the principal. You must consult with an attorney in your state to determine whether a general power of attorney will also authorize the agent to make health care decisions for the principal. In those cases where a durable general power of attorney does not grant authority to the agent to make health care decisions, or where you do not want to give another person the ability to completely manage your affairs, but only want to delegate the ability to make health care decisions for you if you become incompetent, then a durable special power of attorney for health care decisions would be appropriate.

The person you designate as an agent under a durable power of attorney for health care decisions would have the same rights as you the patient would have. This would include a right of access to your medical records and a right to sufficient information about your prognosis, risks of various medical treatments, and possible alternatives to those treatments, so your agent is able to give or withhold informed consent based on your best interests.

When you have a properly executed durable special power of attorney for health care decisions, your physician is bound to follow the directions of your designated agent, or else discontinue as your physician. This special type of power of attorney has some advantages over the living will because there are undoubtedly circumstances for which you would be unable to foresee, and may not have addressed in your living will. With this special power of attorney, you put decisions in the hands of someone you intimately trust, who can listen to and respond to the developments in your case and conditions. It also helps resolve any conflicts or disputes within a family as to who should be your substitute decision maker.

For these reasons, you and your designated agent must completely discuss your wishes, desires, and intentions before you complete this special power of attorney. Your designated agent must understand what choices you want made in various circumstances. For example, what types of medical treatments would you not want to have? Would you want to have tube feedings, a ventilator, or IVs sustain you under certain circumstances? Discuss these questions with your agent before you finally execute the document. Write down your instructions and concerns and go over your living will with your proposed agent so you are convinced your agent would be of the same mind as you are when it came to consenting to or refusing medical care. The agent you specify in your durable special power of attorney for health care decisions may exercise many types of decisions on your behalf. They may range from consent for hospitalization to consent for placement in a nursing home or consent to a surgical operation. If you discuss your wishes on these matters with your agent in advance, your agent will be better equipped to act and carry out your desires.

The following are several examples of special powers of attorney for health care decisions. These are provided as an illustration only and pertain to the jurisdictions indicated. Do to the great divergence in power of attorney laws throughout the country, examples from all fifty states are not provided. All 50 states and the District of Columbia have general durable power of attorney statutes. For your reference, the following are the statutory references to the Durable Power of Attorney statutes for all 50 states: See Ala. Code Section 26-1-2 (1986); Alaska Stat. Ann. Sections 13-26-350 to 13-26-356 (Supp. 1989); Ariz. Rev. Stat. Ann. Section 14-5501 (1975); Ark. Code Ann. Sections 28-68-201 to 28-68-203 (1987); Cal. Civ. Code Ann. Section 2400 (West Supp. 1990); Colo. Rev. Stat. Section 15-14-501 et seq. (1987); Conn. Gen. Stat. Section 45-69o (Supp. 1989); Del. Code Ann., Tit. 12, Section 4901-4905 (1987); D.C. Code Section 21-2081 et. seq. (1989); Fla. Stat. Section 709.08 (1989); Ga. Code Ann. Section 10-6-46 (1989); Haw. Rev. Stat. Sections 551D-1 to 551D-7 (Supp. 1989); Idaho Code Section 15-5-501 et seq. (Supp. 1989). Ill, rev. Stat., ch. 1101/2, Section 802-6 (1987); Ind. Code Sections 30-2-11-1 to 30-2-11-7 (1988); Iowa Code Section 633.705 (Supp. 1989); Kan. Stat. Ann. Section 58-610 (1983); Ky. Rev. Stat. Ann. Sectin 386.093 (Baldwin 1983); La. Civ. Code Ann. Section 3027 (West Supp. 1990); Me. Rev. Stat. Ann., Tit. 18-A, Section 5-501 et seq. (Supp. 1989); Md. Est. & Trusts Code Ann. Section 13-601-13 to 602 (1974) (as interpreted by the Attorney General, see 73 Op. Md. Atty. Gen. No. 88-046 (Oct. 17, 1988)); Mass. Gen. Laws Sections 201B:a to 201B:7 (1988); Mich. Compt. Laws Section 700-495, 70000000.497 (1980); Minn. Stat. Section 523.01 et seq. (1988); Miss. Code Ann. Section 87-3-13 (Supp. 1989). Mo. Rev. Stat. Section 404.700 (Supp. 1990); Mont. Code Ann. Sections 72-5-501 to 72-5-502 (1989); Neb. Rev. Stat. Sections 30-2664 to 30-2672, 30-2667 (1985); Nev. Rev. Stat. Section 111.460 et seq. (1986); N.H. Rev. Stat. Ann. Section 506:6 et seq. (Supp. 1989); N.J. Stat. Ann. Section 46:2B-8 (1989); N.M. Stat. Ann. Section 45-5-501 et seq. (1989); N.Y. Gen. Oblig. Law Section 5-1602 (McKinney 1989); N.C. Gen. Stat. Section 32A-1 et seq. 91987); N.D. Cent. Code Sections 30.1-30 to 01-30.1-30-05 (Supp. 1989); Ohio Rev. Code Ann. Section 1337.09 (SUpp. 1989); Okla. Stat., Tit. 58, Sections 1071-1077 (Supp. 1989). Ore. Rev. Stat. Section 127.005 (1989). Pa. Stat. Ann., Tit. 20, Section 5601 et seq., 5602(a)(9) (Purdon Supp. 1989); R.I. Gen. Laws Section 34-22-6.1 (1984); S.C. Code Sections 62-5-501 to 62-5-502 (1987); S.D. Codified Laws Section 59-7-2.1 (1978); Tenn. Code Ann. Section 34-6-101 et seq. (1984); Tex Prob. Code Ann. Section 36A (Supp. 1990); Utah Code Ann. Section 75-5-501 et seq. (1978); Vt. Stat. Ann., Tit. 14, Section 3051 et seq. (1989). W. Va. Code Section 39-4-1 et seq. (Supp. 1989); Wis. Sta. Section 243.07 (1987-1988); (as interpreted by the Attorney General, see Wis. Op. Atty. Gen. 35-88 91988), Wyo. Stat. Section 3-5-101 e seq. (Supp. 1985).

Consult with your personal attorney for the appropriate form in your home state. Since power of attorneys are regulated by state statute, they are effective only in the state they are issued. As always, if you have any questions regarding the appropriateness or use of a particular form as applied to your particular circumstances, the author strongly encourages you to consult with an attorney.

MONTANA - SPECIAL DURABLE POWER OF ATTORNEY FOR MEDICAL CONSENT

KNOW ALL MEN BY THESE PRESENTS: That the undersigned:

NAME: Lee R. Kerr

ADDRESS: Hysham, MT

has made, constituted and appointed, and by this document does make, constitute and appoint:

NAME: Delnetta J. Kerr

ADDRESS: Hysham, MT

my true and lawful attorney for me and in my name, place and stead, to do and perform all things necessary to make binding decisions concerning my medical treatment and make health care decisions for me. For the purposes of this document, "Health Care Decisions" means consent, refusal of consent, or withdrawal of consent to any care, treatment, service, or procedure to maintain, diagnose, or treat an individual's physical or mental condition.

I do grant and give unto said attorney full authority to do and perform all and every act or thing which may be requisite or necessary to be done, as fully, and to all intents and purpose, as I might or could do if personally present, with full powers of substitution and revocation, hereby ratifying with full powers of substitution and revocation, all that said attorney shall lawfully do or cause to be done by virtue of this instrument.

My above said attorney is granted full authority to inspect and disclose any information pertaining to my mental and physical condition, and is authorized to sign releases, waivers, or documents, including any "refusal of treatment", and/or "release from liability", which may be required by a hospital or physician.

This Power of Attorney shall become effective as of the dated I sign this document and shall not be affected by subsequent disability or incapacity of the principal or lapse of time.

The law of the State of Montana and, in particular, Chapter 72-5-501 et. seq. Montana Code Annotated, and any successor sections thereto, shall govern this power of attorney in all respects.

IN WITNESS WHEREOF, I have hereunto set my hand and seal this 25 day of Sept , 1990.

_____
NAME

STATE OF MONTANA   )
                      : ss.
County of _Treasure_)

On this _25th_ day of _September_, 19_90_, before me, the undersigned
notary public, personally appeared _Lee R. Kerr_, known to me (or
satisfactorily proven) to be the person whose name is subscribed to the
foregoing instrument, and acknowledged that she/he executed the same
for the purpose therein contained.

IN WITNESS WHEREOF, I hereunto set my hand and official seal.

Kathleen Thomas

(SEAL)

Notary Public for the State of Montana
Residing at: _Hysham_
My Commission expires: _January 11, 1991_

SPECIAL POWER OF ATTORNEY - UTAH

I, _____, of _____, this _____ day of _____, 19___, being of sound mind, willfully and voluntarily appoint _____ of _____ as my agent and attorney-in-fact, without substitution, with lawful authority to execute a directive on my behalf under Section 75-2-1105, governing the care and treatment to be administered to or withheld from me at any time after I incur an injury, disease, or illness which renders me unable to give current directions to attending physicians and other providers of medical services.

I understand that "life-sustaining procedures" do not include the administration of medication or sustenance, or the performance of any medical procedure deemed necessary to provide comfort care, or to alleviate pain, unless my attorney-in-fact specifies these procedures be considered life-sustaining.

I have carefully selected my above-named agent with confidence in the belief that his person's familiarity with my desires, beliefs, and attitudes will result in directions to attending physicians and providers of medical services which would probably be the same as I would give if able to do so.

This power of attorney shall be and remain in effect from the time my attending physician certifies that I have incurred a physical or mental condition rendering me unable to give current directions to attending physicians and other providers of medical services as to my care and treatment.

_____
Signature of Principal

STATE OF UTAH   )
                 : ss.
County of _____)

On the _____ day of _____, 19___, personally appeared before me _____, who duly acknowledged to me that he had read and fully understands the foregoing power of attorney, executed the same of his own volition and for the purposes set forth, and that he was acting under no constraint or undue influence whatsoever.

_____
Notary Public

My Commission expires: _____
Residing at: _____

A DURABLE POWER OF ATTORNEY FOR HEALTH CARE - IDAHO

1. DESIGNATION OF HEALTH CARE AGENT.

I, _____, of _____ (address), do hereby designate and appoint _____ (Insert name, address, and telephone number of one individual only as your agent to make health care decisions for you. None of the following may be designated as your agent: (1) your treating health care provider, (2) a nonrelative employee of your treating health care provider, (3) an operator of a community care facility, or (4) a nonrelative employee of an operator of a community care facility).

as my attorney in fact (agent) to make health care decisions for me as authorized in this document. For the purposes of this document, "health care decision" means consent, refusal of consent, or withdrawal of consent to any care, treatment, service, or procedure to maintain, diagnose, or treat an individual's physical condition.

2. CREATION OF DURABLE POWER OF ATTORNEY FOR HEALTH CARE.
By this document I intend to create a durable power of attorney for health care. This power of attorney shall not be affected by my subsequent incapacity.

3. GENERAL STATEMENT OF AUTHORITY GRANTED.
Subject to any limitations in this document, I hereby grant to my agent full power and authority to make health care decisions for me to the same extent that I could make such decisions for myself if I had the capacity to do so. In exercising this authority, my agent shall make health care decisions that are consistent with my desires as stated in this document or otherwise made known to my agent, including, but not limited to, my desires concerning obtaining or refusing or withdrawing life-prolonging care, treatment, services, and procedures. (If you want to limit the authority of your agent to make health care decisions for you, you can state the limitations in paragraph 4 ("Statement of Desires, Special Provisions, and Limitations") below. You can indicate your desires by including a statement of your desires in the same paragraph.)

4. STATEMENT OF DESIRES, SPECIAL PROVISIONS, AND LIMITATIONS.
(Your agent must make health care decisions that are consistent with your known desires. You can, but are not required to, state your desires in the space provided below. You should consider whether you want to include a statement of your desires concerning life-prolonging care, treatment, services, and procedures. You can also include a statement of your desires concerning other matters relating to your health care. You can also make your desires known to your agent by discussing your desires with your agent or by some other means. If there are any types of treatment that you do not want to be used, you should state them in the space below. If you want to limit in any other way the authority given your agent by this document, you should state the limits in the space below. If you do not state any limits, your agent will have broad powers to make health care decisions for you, except to the extent that there are limits provided by law.)

161

In exercising the authority under this durable power of attorney for health care, my agent shall act consistently with my desires as stated below and is subject to the special provisions and limitations stated in the living will. Additional statement of desires, special provisions, and limitations: _____

(You may attach additional pages if you need more space to complete your statement. If you attach additional pages, you must date and sign each of the additional pages at the same time you date and sign this document.)

5. INSPECTION AND DISCLOSURE OF INFORMATION RELATING TO MY PHYSICAL OR MENTAL HEALTH. Subject to any limitations in this document, my agent has the power and authority to do all of the following:

(a) Request, review, and receive any information, verbal or written, regarding my physical or mental health, including, but not limited to, medical and hospital records.

(b) Execute on my behalf any releases or other documents that my be required in order to obtain this information.

(c) Consent to the disclosure of this information.

(d) Consent to the donation of any of my organs for medical purposes. (If you want to limit the authority of your agent to receive and disclose information relating to your health, you must state the limitations in paragraph 4 ("Statement of Desires, Special Provisions, and Limitations") above.)

6. SIGNING DOCUMENTS, WAIVERS, AND RELEASES. Where necessary to implement the health care decisions that my agent is authorized by this document to make, my agent has the power and authority to execute on my behalf all of the following:

(a) Documents titled or purporting to be a "Refusal to Permit Treatment" and "Leaving Hospital Against Medical Advice."

(b) Any necessary waiver or release from liability required by a hospital or physician.

7. DESIGNATION OF ALTERNATE AGENTS. (You are not required to designate any alternate agents but you may do so. Any alternate agent you designate will be able to make the same health care decisions as the agent you designated in paragraph 1, above, in the event that agent is unable or ineligible to act as your agent. If the agent you designated is your spouse, he or she becomes ineligible to act as your agent if your marriage is dissolved.)

If the person designated as my agent in paragraph 1 is not available or becomes ineligible to act as my agent to make a health care decision for me or loses the mental capacity to make health care decisions for me, or if I revoke that person's appointment or authority to act as my agent to make health care decisions for me, then I designate and appoint the following persons to serve as my agent to make health care decisions for me as authorized in this document, such persons to serve in the order listed below:

A. First Alternate Agent _____
(Insert name, address, and telephone number of first alternate agent)

162

B. Second Alternate Agent _____
   (Insert name, address, and telephone number of second alternate
   agent)

   8. PRIOR DESIGNATIONS REVOKED. I revoke any prior durable power
of attorney for health care.

DATE AND SIGNATURE OF PRINCIPAL
(You Must Date and Sign This Power of Attorney)

   I sign my name to this Statutory Form Durable Power of Attorney
for Health Care on _____ (Date) at _____, (City) _____. (State)

_____
(You sign here)

(This Power of Attorney will not be valid unless it is signed by two
qualified witnesses who are present when you sign or acknowledge your
signature. If you have attached any additional pages to this form, you
must date and sign each of the additional pages at the same time you
date and sign this Power of Attorney.)

STATEMENT OF WITNESSES

   (This document must be witnessed by two qualified adult witnesses.
None of the following may be used as a witness: (1) a person you
designate as your agent or alternate agent, (2) a health care provider,
(3) an employee of a health care provider, (4) the operator of a
community care facility, (5) an employee of an operator of a community
care facility. At least one of the witnesses must make the additional
declaration set out following the place where the witnesses sign.)
   I declare under penalty of perjury under the laws of Idaho that
the person who signed or acknowledged this document is personally known
to me (or proved to me on the basis of convincing evidence) to be the
principal, that the principal signed or acknowledged this durable power
of attorney in my presence, that the principal appears to be of sound
mind and under no duress, fraud, or undue influence, that I am not the
person appointed as attorney in fact by this document, and that I am
not a health care provider, an employee of a health care provider, the
operator of a community care facility, nor an employee of an operator
of a community care facility.

Signature: _____
Print Name: _____
Date: _____ Residence Address: _____

Signature: _____
Print Name: _____

Date: _____ Residence Address: _____

(At least one of the above witnesses must also sign)

I further declare under penalty of perjury under the laws of Idaho that I am not related to the principal by blood, marriage, or adoption, and, to the best of my knowledge, I am not entitled to any part of the estate of the principal upon the death of the principal under a will now existing or by operation of law.

Signature: _____
Signature: _____

NOTARY

(Signer of instrument may either have it witnessed as above or have his/her signature notarized as below, to legalize this instrument.)

State of Idaho   )
) ss.
County of _____)

On this ____ day of _____, 19___, before me personally appeared _____ (full name of signer of instrument) to be known (or proved to me on basis of satisfactory evidence) to be the person whose name is subscribed to this instrument, and acknowledged that he/she executed it. I declare under penalty of perjury that the person whose name is subscribed to this instrument appears to be of sound mind and under no duress, fraud or undue influence.

_____
(Signature of Notary)

MONTANA DECLARATION FOR HEALTH CARE PROXY

Section 50-9-103 (3). A declaration that designates another individual to make decisions governing the withholding or withdrawal of life-sustaining treatment may, but need not, be in the following form:

DECLARATION

If I should have an incurable and irreversible condition that, without the administration of life-sustaining treatment, will, in the opinion of my attending physician, cause my death within a relatively short time and I am no longer able to make decisions regarding my medical treatment, I appoint _____ or, if he or she is not reasonably available or is unwilling to serve, _____, to make decisions on my behalf regarding withholding or withdrawal of treatment that only prolongs the process of dying and is not necessary for my comfort or to alleviate pain, pursuant to the Montana Rights of the Terminally Ill Act.

If the individual I have appointed is not reasonably available or is unwilling to serve, I direct my attending physician, pursuant to the Montana Rights of the Terminally Ill Act, to withhold or withdraw treatment that only prolongs the process of dying and is not necessary for my comfort or to alleviate pain.

Signed this _____ day of _____, 19___.

Signature_____

City, County, and State of Residence_____

The declarant voluntarily signed this document in my presence.

_____   _____
Witness   Witness

_____   _____
Address   Address

Name and address of designee.

_____
Name

_____
Address

CONCLUSION

As you come to this point, hopefully you have completed the three basic steps necessary to prevent a needless tragedy in your future. You have prepared a statutory living will, a declaration of intent regarding limiting or refusing medical consent, and a durable power of attorney for health care decisions. These three steps will be accomplished in either one, two, or three separate legal documents, depending upon the status of the law of your particular state, and the advice of your attorney after consultation.

Although a living will is an imperfect document that has difficulty in addressing all possible contingencies, the Supreme Court of this great land has placed the burden upon you to make clear advance directives if you hope to avoid the horrors of unwanted medical treatment. Following the steps outlined in this book, including the special durable power of attorney for health care decisions, will help fill in any gaps currently existing in present living will statutes, and give you the maximum protection currently available under existing law to protect your right to a natural death with dignity.

NATURAL DEATH WITH DIGNITY:

PROTECTING YOUR RIGHT TO REFUSE MEDICAL TREATMENT

CHAPTER 7 —

SUPPLEMENTAL READING, REFERENCES, AND RESOURCES

"Artificial Nutrition and the Terminally Ill: How Should Washington Decide?" 61 Washington Law Review 419 (April 1986)

"Balancing the Right to Die With Competing Interests: A Socio-Legal Enigma." 13 Pepperdine Law Review 109 (Dec. 1985)

"The Barber Decision: A Questionable Approach to Termination of Life-Support Systems for the Patient in a Persistent Vegetative State." 15 Golden Gate University Law Review 371 (Summer 1985)

"The Bell Tolls for Thee: But When? Legal Acceptance of Brain Death as a Criteria for Death." 9 American Journal of Trial Advocacy 331 (Fall 1985)

Beschle. "Autonomous Decisionmaking and Social Choice: Examining the Right to Die." 77 Kentucky Law Journal 319 (Winter 1988/89)

Beyer. "The Right to Privacy - The Right To Die." 54 Inter Alia F1 (March / April 1989)

Bopp. "Is Assisted Suicide Constitutionally Protected." 3 Issues in Law and Medicine 113 (Fall 1987)

_____. "Nutrition and Hydration for Patients: The Constitutional Aspects." 4 Issues in Law and Medicine 3 (Summer 1988)

Bostrom. "Euthanasia in the Netherlands: A Model for the United States?" 4 Issues in Law and Medicine 467 (Spring 1989)

Bradley. "Does Autonomy Require Informed and Specific Refusal of Life-Sustaining Medical Treatment?" 5 Issues in Law and Medicine 301 (Winter 1989)

Brown. "Medical Decision-Making At the End of Life." 67 Michigan Bar Journal 1106 (Nov. 1988)

Cantor. "Conroy, Best Interests, and the Handling of Dying Patients." 37 Rutgers Law Review 543 (Spring 1985)

Cerminara. "Refusing Life-Sustaining Treatment for Incompetent Patients: Mere Existence or a Quality LIfe?" 35 Medical Trial Technique Quarterly 121 (1989 Annual)

Chapman. "The Uniform Rights of the Terminally Ill Act: Too Little, Too Late?" 42 Arkansas Law Review 319 (Spring 1989)

"Choosing How to Die: The Need for Reform of Oregon's Living Will Legislation." 23 Willamette Law Review 69 (Winter 1987)

Cohen, Cynthia B. Casebook on the Termination of Life-Sustaining Treatment and the Care of the Dying. Bloomington: Indiana University

Press, c1988.

Cole, Harry A.   One In a Million.   Boston: Little, Brown, c1990.

Coleman.   "Assisted Suicide: An Ethical Perspective."   3 Issues in Law and Medicine 267 (Winter 1987)

Collins.   "The Foundations of the Right to Die."   90 West Virginia Law Review 235 (Fall 1987)

"Comparison of the Living Will Statutes of the Fifty States." 14 Journal of Contemporary LAw 105 (1988)

Cooper. "Playing God: Bioethicists, A New Class of Consultants, Juggle Principles of Law, medicine and Philosophy."   9 California Lawyer 24 (Nov. 1989)

Cox.   "Government As Arbiter, Not Custodian: Relational Privacy As Foundation for a Right To Refuse Medical Treatment Prolonging Incompetents' Lives."   18 New Mexico Law Review 131 (Winter 1988)

Davenport.   "The Right to Die: Sources of Information."   5 Legal Reference Services Quarterly 47 (Spring 1985)

Doty.   "Allowing the Dying Child To Die; Who Decides?"   3 Washington Lawyer 36 (March / April 1989)

"Effect of Incarceration on the Right to Die."   11 New England Journal on Criminal and Civil Confinement 395 (Summer 1985)

"Equality for the Elderly Incompetent: A Proposal for Dignified Death." 39 Stanford Law Review 689 (Feb. 1987)

"Findings of Fact and Conclusions of Law Denying Preliminary Injunction."   4 Issues of Law and Medicine 129 (Summer 1988)

Fisher.   "The Suicide Trap: Bouvia v. Superior Court and the Right to Refuse Medical Treatment. (Case Note)"   21 Loyola of Los Angeles Law Review 219 (Nov. 1987)

Francis.   "The Evanescence of Living Wills."   24 Real Property, Probate, and Trust Journal 141 (Spring 1989)

Garrard.   "A Look at Indiana's Living Will Statute: Right to Forego Medical Treatment."   30 Res Gestae 13 (July 1986)

Geffand.   "Living Will Statutes: The First Decade."   1987 Wisconsin Law Review 737 (Sept / Oct. 1987)

Goldberg.   "Choosing Life After Death: Respecting Religious and Moral Convictions in Near Death Decisions." 39 Syracuse Law Review 1197 (Winter 1988)

Greengard.   "The Last Rights. (Right to Die)"   12 Barrister 4 (Summer 1985)

<u>Guidelines on the Termination of Life-Sustaining Treatment and the Care of the Dying: A Report</u>. Briarcliff Manor, N.Y.: Hastings Center, c1987.

Hallagan. "Natural Death Acts and Right to Die Legislation." 32 <u>Medical Trial Technique Quarterly</u> 301 (1986 Annual)

Handler. "Social Dilemmas, Judicial (Ir) resolution." 40 <u>Rutgers Law Review</u> 1 (Fall 1987)

Harber. "Withholding Food and Water from a Patient: Should it Be Condoned in California?" 16 <u>Pacific Law Journal</u> 877 (April 1985)

"Hold on Courts: May a Comatose Patient be Denied Food and Water." 31 <u>Saint Louis University Law Journal</u> 749 (Sept. 1987)

Horan, Dennis J. <u>Death, Dying and Euthanasia</u>. Washington: University Publications of America, 1977.

Ikuta. "Dying at the Right Time: A Critical Legal Theory Approach to Timing-Of-Death Issues." 5 <u>Issues in Law and Medicine</u> 3 (Summer 1989)

Ingram. "State Interference with Religiously Motivated Decisions on Medical Treatment." 93 <u>Dickinson Law Review</u> 41 (Fall 1988)

Jorrie. "The Tax Advantages of Lingering Death." 48 <u>Texas Bar Journal</u> 1070 (Oct. 1985)

Joyce. "To Die Or Not to Die: The New York Legislature Ponders a Natural Death Act." 13 <u>Fordham Urban Law Journal</u> 639 (Summer 1985)

Keilitz. "Decisionmaking in Authorizing and Withholding Life Sustaining Medical Treatment: From Quinlan to Cruzan." 13 <u>Mental and Physical Disability Law Reporter</u> 482 (Sept Oct. 1989)

Kirkpatrick. "In Re Jobes (Treatment Decisions May Be Made By a Surrogate Decisionmaker When the Patient Has Not Left Clear Evidence of His Own Intent)" 3 <u>Issues in Law and Medicine</u> 183 (Fall 1987)

Loop. "Decisions at the End of LIfe." 5 <u>Issues in Law and Medicine</u> 225 (Fall 1989)

Kronmiller. "A Necessary Compromise: The Right to Forego Artificial Nutrition and Hydration under Maryland's Life Sustaining Procedures Act." 47 <u>Maryland Law Review</u> 1188 (Summer 1988)

Lanza. "Family law - Right to Die - Vegetative Patient's Right to Self-Determination Permits Surrogate Decision-Maker to Terminate Artificial Feeding. (Case Note)" 18 <u>Seton Hall Law Review</u> 458 (Spring 1988)

Leavitt. "A Prisoner's Right To Die - The Factor of Intent. (Case Note)" 37 <u>Maine Law Review</u> 447 (July 1985)

Marsh. "Living Will LEgislation in Colorado: An Analysis of the Colorado Medical Treatment Decision Act in Relation to Similiar Developments in Other Jurisdictions." 63 Denver University Law Review 5 (1987)

Matuschak. "The Right to Decline Medical Treatment after Brophy." 32 Boston Bar Journal 25 (July / Aug. 1988)

McHugh, James T. Death, Dying, and the Law. Huntington, Ind.: Our Sunday Visitor, c1976.

Meyers, David W. Medico-Legal Implication of Death and Dying: A Detailed Discussion of the Medical and Legal Implications Involved in Death and/or Care of the Dying and Terminal Patient. Rochester: Layers Co-Operative Publishing Co., 1981.

Miller. "Legislative Initiatives on Life-Sustaining Treatment; The Do-Not-Resuscitate Law and the Health Care Proxy Proposal." 61 New York State Bar Journal 30 (February 1989)

_____. "Right-To-Die Damage Actions: Developments in the Law." 65 Denver University Law Review 181 (Winter / Spring 1988)

Miltenberger. "The Dilemma of the Person in a Persistent Vegetative State: A Plea tot he Legislature for Help." 54 Missouri Law Review 645 (Summer 1989)

Mooney. "Deciding Not to Resuscitate Hospital Patients: Medical and Legal Perspectives." 1986 University of Illinois Law Review 1025 (1986)

Morgan. "Constitutional Development of Judicial Criteria in Right-To-Die Cases: From brain Dead to Persistent Vegetative State." 23 Wake Forest Law Review 721 (Dec. 1988)

Murphy. "A New Form of Medical Malpractice?: Missouri's Living Will Statute." 42 Journal of the Missouri Bar 11 (Jan / Feb. 1986)

Myers. "Health Care Provider Civil Liability for Denying Life-Sustaining Treatment." 55 Defense Counsel Journal 301 (July 1988)

O'Brien. "Facilitating Euthanatic, Rational Suicide: Help Me Go Gentle Into That Good NIght." 31 Saint Louis University Law Journal 655 (Sept. 1987)

Oddi. "The Tort of Interference with the Right to Die: The Wrongful Living Cause of Action." 75 Georgetown Law Journal 625 (Dec. 1986)

"Ohio's Need to Enact a Living Will Statute and Recognize the Terminally Ill Patient's Right to Death with Dignity." 19 Akron Law Review 463 (Winter 1986)

Orenstein. "Minnesota's Living Will ..." 46 Bench and Bar of

<u>Minnesota</u> 21 (August 1989)

Oxman. "In Re Joseph V. Gardner: The Balance Between Patient Rights to Self-Determination and the State's Responsibility To Preserve life." 4 <u>Maine Bar Journal</u> 10 (Jan. 1989)

Postell. "The Right To Die: Who Decides?" 21 <u>Trial</u> 68 (May 1985)

Poston. "Who Speaks for the Comatose?" 23 <u>Arizona Bar Journal</u> 14 (Feb / March 1988)

Potts. "Looking for the Exit Door: Killing and Caring in Modern Medicine." 25 <u>Houston Law Review</u> 493 (May 1988)

Raiche. "Is Living Will the Best Revenge?: New Hampshire's Living Will Statute." 28 <u>New Hampshire Bar Journal</u> 45 (Fall 1986)

Reidinger. "Choosing Life: Limiting the Right to Die." 75 <u>ABA Journal</u> 83 (January 1989)

Rhoden. "Litigating Life and Death." 102 <u>Harvard Law Review</u> 375 (Dec. 1988)

Richard. "Someone Make Up My Mind: The Troubling Right To Die Issues Presented by Incompetent Patients with No Prior Expression of a Treatment Preference." 64 <u>Notre Dame Law Review</u> 394 (Summer 1989)

Riga, Peter J. <u>Right to Die or Right to Live? Legal Aspects of Dying and Death</u>. Gaithersburg, MD.: Associated Faculty Press, c1983.

"The Right of the Terminally Ill to Die, with Assistance If Necessary." 8 <u>Criminal Justice Journal</u> 403 (1986)

"Right to Refuse Treatment." 4 <u>Behavioral Sciences & the Law</u> 247 (Summer 1986)

<u>Rights of the Terminally Ill</u>. Helena, Mont.:" State Bar of Montana, 1985.

Robertson, John A. <u>The Rights of the Critically Ill: the Basic ACLU Guide to the Rights of Critically Ill and Dying Patients</u>. New York: Bantam Books, 1983.

Robinson. "The Right of An Incompetent To Terminate Life-Supporting Medical Treatment." 77 <u>Illinois Bar Journal</u> 432 (April 1989)

Rothenberg. "Foregoing Life-Sustaining Treatment: What Are the Legal Limits in an Aging Society?" 33 <u>Saint Louis University Law Journal</u> 575 (Spring 1989)

Rubin. "Refusal of Life-Sustaining Treatment for Terminally Ill Incompetent Patients: Court orders and an Alternative." 19 <u>Columbia Journal of Law & Social Problems</u> 19 (Summer 1985)

_____. "When Ethics Collide: Enforcement of Institutional Policies of

Non-Participation in the Termination of Life Sustaining Treatment." 41 Rutgers Law Review 399 (Fall 1988)

Runner. "Constitutional Law ... In Refusing Blood Transfusions ... " 27 Journal of Family Law 524 (February 1989)

Schaeffer. "Death with Dignity: Proposed Amendments to the California Natural Death Act." 25 San Diego Law Review 781 (Sept / Oct. 1988)

Scheb. "Termination of Life Support Systems for Minor Children: Evolving Legal Responses." 54 Tennessee Law Review 1 (Fall 1986)

Schimke. "The Natural Death Act: Protection for the Right to Die." 47 Montana Law Review 379 (Summer 1986)

Segers. "Elderly Persons on the Subject of Euthanasia (Euthanasia in the Netherlands)." 3 Issues in Law and Medicine 407 (Spring 1988)

Showalter, J. Stuart. To Treat or Not to Treat: a Working Document for Making Critical Life Decisions. St. Louis: Catholic Health Association of the United States, c1984.

Sloan, Irving J. The Right to Die: Legal and Ethical Problems. New York: Oceana, 1988.

Smith. "All's Well That Ends Well: Toward a Policy of Assisted Rational Suicide or Merely Enlightened Self-Determination?" 22 U.C. Davis Law Review 275 (Winter 1989)

Smith. "The Expense of Expanding the Right to Die: A Trilogy." 5 Georgia State University Law Review 117 (Fall 1988)

Sondag. "In Re Farrell (A Mentally Competent Patient can Choose to Have a Respirator Discontinued)." 3 Issues in Law and Medicine 171 (Fall 1987)

Stone. "The Right to Die: New Problems for Law and Medicine and Psychiatry." 37 Emory Law Journal 627 (Summer 1988)

Taylor. "The 1989 Living Will Amendment - Durable Power of Attorney for Health Care." 18 Colorado Lawyer 1321 (July 1989)

United States. President's Commission for the Study of Ethical Problems in Medicine and Biomedical and Behavioral Research. Deciding to Forego LIfe-Sustaining Treatment: A Report on the Ethical, Medical, and Legal Issues in Treatment Decisions. Washington: The Commission, 1983.

VanDerhoef. "Where Does Washington Stand on Artificial Nutrition and Hydration? (Case Note)" 13 University of Puget Sound Law Review 197 (Fall 1989)

Veroneau. "Withdrawing Medical Care from Persistently Vegetative Patients. (Case Note)" 41 Maine Law Review 447 (July 1989)

Vile. "Living Wills in New York: Are They Valid?" 38 Syracuse Law Review 1369 (Winter 1987)

Vitiello. "Louisiana's Natural Death Act and Dilemmas in Medical Ethics." 46 Louisiana Law Review 529 (Nov. 1985)

Weinberg. "Whose Right Is It Anyway? Individualism, Community, and the Right To Die: A Commentary on the New Jersey Experience." 40 Hastings Law Journal 119 (Nov. 1988)

Wentworth. "Termination of Life-Prolonging Medical Treatment: An Analysis of Pennsylvania's Proposed Medical Treatment Decision Act." 92 Dickinson Law Review 839 (Summer 1988)

Winslade, William J. Choosing LIfe or Death: A Guide for Patients, Families, and Professionals. New York: Free Press, c1986.

_____. "Guarding the Exit Door: A Plea for Limited Toleration of Euthanasia." 25 Houston Law Review 517 (May 1988)

"Withdrawal of Nutrition and Hydration from Incompetent patients in Missouri." 54 Missouri Law Review 731 (Summer 1989)

Wolf. "Florida Living Will." 59 Florida Bar Journal 13 (April 1985)

Wong, Cynthia B. Dilemmas of Dying: Policies and Procedures for Decisions Not to Treat: Proceedings of a 1979 Conference Sponsored by Medicine in the Public Interest, Inc. Boston: Hall Medical, c1981

Woodruff. "Letting Life Run Its Course: Do-Not-Resuscitate Orders and Withdrawal of Life-Sustaining Treatment." 1989 Army Lawyer 6 (April 1989)

Zinberg. "Decisions for the Dying: An Empirical Study of Physicians' Responses to Advance Directives." 13 Vermont Law Review 445 (Winter 1989)

INDEX

ORDER FORM

HELP AWAKEN OTHERS! GIVE <u>NATURAL DEATH WITH DIGNITY</u> TO FRIENDS, RELATIVES, NEIGHBORS, CLERGYMEN, DOCTORS, NURSES, TEACHERS, LIBRARIES. DO YOUR PART IN THIS VITAL EDUCATIONAL JOB. ORDER COPIES OF <u>NATURAL DEATH WITH DIGNITY</u> FOR YOUR OWN USE, AT THE LOW QUANTITY PRICES BELOW.

QUANTITY PRICES

	SOFTBOUND ED.	HARDBOUND ED.
1 copy	$19.95ea.	$29.95ea.
5 copies	$18.95ea.	$28.95ea.
10 copies	$17.95ea.	$27.95ea.
25 copies	$16.95ea.	$26.95ea.
100 copies	$14.95ea.	$24.95ea.
500 copies	$12.95ea.	$20.95ea.
1000 copies	$8.98ea.	$13.35ea.

YES! I want to avoid the agony of unwanted health care. Please send me _____ softbound copies and _____ hardbound copies of <u>Natural Death With Dignity</u> with forms and instructions to limit or refuse medical consent. Enclosed is $_____. (Send check or money order.) OR-

WE ACCEPT VISA or MASTERCARD

ORDER BY PHONE

CALL 1-800-447-KERR (5377)

9 A.M. TO 5 P.M., MON.-FRI. MOUNTAIN TIME

Method of Payment by Mail-

___ Enclosed is my check or Money Order.
___ Please charge to my credit card.
___ Visa   ___ MasterCard
Card No._____
Exp. Date_____ Phone No._____
X_____
Signature

_____
P.O. Box or Street

_____
City, State, Zip Code